Patrick H. Redmond

History of Quincy and Its Men of Mark

Or, Facts and Figures Exhibiting Its Advantages and Resources, Manufactures and Commerce

Patrick H. Redmond

History of Quincy and Its Men of Mark
Or, Facts and Figures Exhibiting Its Advantages and Resources, Manufactures and Commerce

ISBN/EAN: 9783337112004

Printed in Europe, USA, Canada, Australia, Japan

Cover: Foto ©ninafisch / pixelio.de

More available books at **www.hansebooks.com**

HISTORY OF QUINCY,

AND

ITS MEN OF MARK,

OR

Facts and Figures exhibiting its Advantages and Resources, Manufactures and Commerce.

BY PAT. H. REDMOND.

QUINCY:
HEIRS & RUSSELL, BOOK AND JOB PRINTERS, WEST SIDE WASHINGTON PARK.
1869.

PREFACE.

After devoting a large share of time and labor to this work, the author offers it to the public not as a complete history of Quincy, but as the best that he was enabled under the circumstances to compile. The effort to furnish a detailed review of the commerce and manufactures of a city of Quincy's size, is necessarily attended with greater difficulty and labor than would such an undertaking in the great cities of the Union, where Boards of Trade flourish, and where statistics of the manufactures and sales of every department are annually prepared and preserved for reference. Yet, notwithstanding, the want of such facilities for obtaining information has been seriously felt, and added materially to our labors, we have still, through the assistance of our leading business men, obtained accurate statistics of the transactions in most of the important departments, and submit them to the citizens of Quincy and to our readers generally, as an evidence of the prosperity which has been wrought by the energy, enterprise and determination of our business men.

For much, and in fact most of the information here submitted, we are of course indebted to the old residents of Quincy, who have grown with it, and whose industry, ability, and public spirit carried it safely through all the vicissitudes, from a frontier settlement to a prosperous and wealthy city.

The biographies here given to the public will be recognized by many as truthful sketches of leading and influential citizens, who by their sagacity and perseverance carved out their own fortunes, and will enable those not familiar with the progress of Quincy to form an idea of the men to whom she is indebted for her present position as a commercial and manufacturing center.

HISTORICAL.

There is perhaps no city of Quincy's size and population in the Union of which there has been so little said or published, and around whose early history cluster so many recollections and events worthy of being perpetuated. In the rush and turmoil of business our citizens have always had a leisure moment to give to every enterprise that promised to advance the religious, educational or commercial interests of Quincy; but it seems seldom to have occurred to them that by liberally and judiciously heralding the beauties and advantages of their "Model City" our population could be largely augmented, and every department of business vastly benefited.

What we have failed to do in our own behalf, others very naturally have left undone, until we find that it is only within a few years that the outside world has formed any adequate idea of the important interests centered here. The flourishing City of Quincy, when it boasted a population of 20,000 was comparatively unknown, and it was not until that population had increased to nearly 30,000 souls that we commenced to loom up in the eyes of the commercial world, and began to attract a small degree of attention. But while we exhibited enterprise in every other respect, it was not to our enterprise in this line that we owed the first discovery of our importance as a thriving business community by the world at large. With a singular want of sagacity, we allowed our city, with all its advantages and attractions, to slumber quietly on the bank of the great Mississippi, without sounding its merits to the thousands of thrifty emigrants who were journeying westward from the densely populated east, and the other thousands who came with every breeze across the broad Atlantic to find homes of peace and plenty.

Other points, although perhaps not less modest than ourselves, with a wondrous degree of enterprise in this particular role, advantaged themselves of the lethargy that pervaded Quincy and Quincyites, and sang the virtues and 'vantages of their respective localities in most alluring strains. They pictured in the brightest colors their rivers and lakes, their hills and vales, their prairies and forests, and all else that went to make up "The Promised Land of the West," while we reclined here upon the lofty banks of the grand old "Father of Waters," in the midst of the famous "Military Tract," which stretched out a vast expanse of undulating hills and prairies, diversified with stately forests and meandering brooks, that made up the "fairest picture the sun ever shone on."

But while we employed none of the arts of bold speculators to advance the interests of our city or its inhabitants, fate determined that we were not to sink into oblivion, but rather forced upon us a brighter destiny.

The wheels of commerce cycled round, and Quincy, with a firm elastic step marched on in the line of progress. With scarce an effort in her own behalf, prosperity seemed to settle upon her as a favorite spot, and every enterprise to which she gave birth speedily became a success, and resulted handsomely to the originators.

Not one of the would be rivals of the "Gem City" that vauntingly raised their heads as rivals twenty years ago, now presume to contend with us. Hannibal, Keokuk, Peoria, &c., all yield to Quincy the palm for superiority and eminence in population, manufactures, and commerce, and in the great State of Illinois, Chicago alone, the metropolitan wonder of the century, leads, our thriving city.

The progress of Quincy has been steady and unimpeded from the day the first white man trod its prolific soil to the present; and considering the utter absence of ostentation or display regarding our achievements in science, commerce and manufactures, it is not strange that our city has not been better known throughout the Union, and awarded its proper rank among the leading manufacturing and commercial centers. But while we realize that other cities have taken lead of Quincy in parading their advantages to the world, we also recognize the fact, that within a few years we have commenced a system of advertising that promises not only to introduce our city to the country at large, but insures us speedy communication with the outside world. Under the lead of wise and sagacious business men we have turned our attention to perfecting the system of railroads that centers here, and which has been such a powerful ally in developing the resources of the country surrounding us, and thereby building up our city. In substantial enterprises of this nature, which promise permanent advantage to Quincy, our citizens have ever been active and energetic; and this after all is the truest index to the character of any people. Judging our population then in this light, they have shown a world of zeal and public spirit in building here a city of as magnificent proportions and beautiful arrangement as Quincy. Not alone have they profusely expended capital and labor in the construction of its railroads and other facilities of commerce; the erection of its stately business edifices, elegant residences, costly churches and noble educational institutions; but with commendable pride, they have kept an eye to its beauty as well as prosperity. Its broad streets are laid out with faultless regularity, its parks are genial and inviting; its costly mansions and humble cottages are surrounded by capacious yards, modeled after comely designs to enhance the beauties of nature; and everywhere are to be found the evidences of that refined taste and delicate skill, whose exercise has won for Quincy such appellations as "Gem City," "Model City," &c. Added to the natural beauties of location, and the artificial embellishments wrought here by enterprise and skill, Quincy stands pre-eminent among her sisters of the great west for the extent of her public improvements, salubrity of climate, facilities of education, and general eligibility of location as a place of residence.

Our object in issuing this work, has been to better introduce this favored city to those who are seeking a home, where industry and energy are a sure guarantee of prosperity and success: and in doing this we have endeavored to dissemminate abroad only correct information as to her advantages, growth, size, resources and wealth.

It is not our aim or expectation to do full justice to the subject, but simply to enumerate a few of her present and prospective advantages as a manufacturing and commercial point, and to give a brief account of her mercantile and manufacturing interests at the present time.

However, before detailing the operations in business and commerce of the year about to close, it is proper that we should trace Quincy from its first settlement, through the various stages of its existence up to the present time, when it puts forth its claims to metropolitan dignities, and stands erect a full fledged city of 38,000 inhabitants.

"Quincy was originally selected as a town site in the year 1821 by the Hon. John Wood, Ex Governor of the State, who visited this neighborhood in the fall of that year, in company with two others named Moffit and Flinn, in order to look for and examine some land belonging to the latter, and which is now within the city limits. He was so impressed with the beauty of the spot, and so well satisfied that from its geographical position it must become the great point of outlet for the immense productions, which must speedily follow emigration to this and neighboring counties, that he determined in his own words to "settle here for life." He returned in the fall of the succeeding year and erected the first house within the present bounds of Quincy. It was a primitive structure built without the aid of nails or sawed lumber, but unpretending as it was, the associations hanging over it, the almost miraculous changes that have taken place in the face of the country surrounding it, and the marked vicissitudes attending the fortunes of the adventurous pioneer who constructed it, invest it at this day with a halo of interest peculiarly its own, and the mind loves to linger upon it as the germ planted in the wilds of the West, from which has sprung the present vigorous growth of our Model City.

In the spring succeeding Mr. Wood's arrival, Major Jeremiah Rose, a native of New York, came with his family and shared his cabin, Mrs. Rose being the first white woman, and her daughter, now Mrs. George W. Brown, the first white child, residing in Quincy. The next house was built in the spring of 1824 by Mr. Willard Keyes, a native of Vermont, and a former acquaintance of Mr. Wood, and the third in the following fall by John Droulard, a Frenchman. At this time there was no white settlement in the Military Tract north of Gilead, a point sixty miles south of Quincy, (then called Cole's Point) near the centre of Calhoun County, and but two other white men, by name Perigo and Lile, in the bounds of what now is Adams County, and U. S. Troops were stationed at Fort Edwards, the present site of Warsaw, a point forty miles north of Quincy, for the protection of the frontier from the depredations of the Indians who lived in large numbers in the neighborhood. Our pioneers were obliged to go forty miles to mill, but a Dr. Baker, who settled in the fall of 1824 on the creek two miles south of Mr. Wood's house, in order to obviate this inconvenience, with Yankee ingenuity, constructed a machine for pounding corn, the motive of which was water. Placing the grain in a mortar, an industrious pestle soon reduced it to a state suited to manufacture into very tolerable "hoe cakes." A tragical incident connected with the history of this "the first grist mill in Quincy," should not be omitted. One night when "der machine" was in active operation, an unsophisticated coon instigated by the gnawings of hunger, or perhaps by motives of curiosity, attempted to penetrate into its hidden recessess. The descending pestle gave him a forcible intimation that his presence was undesired, and knocking him into the mortar, it continued to pound him with hearty good will until morning, by which time we may conclude that his spirit of exploration was effectually subdued. The condition of the "grist" may "be more easily imagined than described."

Previous to the establishment of the white settlement, an Indian village of the "Sauk" tribe occupied the site of Quincy, and for several years after its establishment the original natives remained in the vicinity, but as a general thing were not troublesome neighbors.

In the fall of 1824, John Wood inserted in a newspaper printed at Edwardsville, called the *Edwardsville Spectator*, a notice that application would be made to the next Legislature for the establishment of a new county, defining its boundaries. In accordance with this application, by an act approved January 13, 1825, the Legislature provided for the organization of Adams County, fixing its boundaries as described in the notice, and as they now exist. Three commissioners were appointed to locate the County Seat, Seymour Kellogg, of Morgan county, Joel Wright, of Montgomery county, and David Dutton of Pike county, who after traveling through and attentively examining the county, decided upon this spot as the one best calculated for the future convenience and accommodation of the people. They christened the new town Quincy, in honor of the President, and, although the ceremonies were not of the most imposing character, thenceforth the city of three log cabins rejoiced in a name.

The first election of officers for Adams County was held on the second day of July, A. D. 1825, when forty votes were polled. Willard Keyes, Levi Wells and Peter Journey were elected County Commissioners, and at their first meeting, during the same month Henry H. Snow was appointed Clerk. This gentleman, pursuant to an order dated November 9th, 1825, was employed to survey and draw plats of the town, and two hundred and thirty lots, ninety-nine by a hundred and ninety-eight feet were laid off. Much of the subsequent prosperity of the place may be ascribed to the wisdom and taste displayed in this survey. Streets were laid off sixty-six feet wide, all but Maine Street, which is eighty-two and a half feet wide, and crossing each other at right angles. A space four hundred feet square was reserved in the center of the town for a public square, now, called Washington Square, and the enclosure which is now Jefferson Square was set apart for a public Cemetery.

The first sale of town lots took place on the thirteenth day of December following, when fifty-one lots which had previously been advertised in the St. Louis and Edwardsville papers, were sold at public auction by the County Commissioners, the major part of which were purchased by the commissioners themselves, the sheriff and other citizens of the County, very few being sold to outside speculators, and thus the curse which has weighed so heavily on other western towns was avoided.

From the close of the year 1825 until the beginning of the year 1835, the growth of Quincy was not rapid. A variety of causes combined to produce this result. Many miles distant from mills, and from any point where provisions or supplies of any kind could be obtained, her residents were obliged to dispense with many of those articles, which are considered, in older communities, as among the "necessaries of life." Their coffee was a decoction of okro seed, an herb cultivated by them for that purpose, and which they sweetened with wild honey, found in great abundance in the neighboring woods. Their nearest blacksmith's shop was at Atlas, forty miles distant, where they carried their plows to be sharpened, swung upon a horse's back. These, and other privations incident to pioneer life, together with several visitations of epidemic disease, during the interval mentioned, prevented any great improvement.

In the spring of 1826, Mr. Asher Anderson arrived with a stock of goods from Maryland and opened the first store, and in the fall of the same year a Court House was built of hewed logs, on the corner of Maine and Fifth streets, and in this building the first school was organized and kept.

In 1828 Charles Holmes and Robert Tillson arrived and established themselves as merchants, and in the succeeding year, 1829, they erected for their accommodation the first frame building in Quincy.

During this and the succeeding year several other

stores were opened by different individuals, and the first steam flour mill was erected by Mr. J. T. Holmes, and put an end for a time to the importation of flour.

In the year 1832 the Black Hawk War broke out, but its chief effect upon Quincy was to increase the number in military titles, as "Colonel," "Major," &c., which it bestowed upon the citizens with a liberal hand.

In 1833 the first regular church was organized, numbering fifteen members.

In June, 1834, the town was incorporated, and Messrs. A. Williams, Jos. T. Holmes, S. W. Rogers, Levi Wells, and Michael Mast were elected trustees. From this period may be dated the rapid advancement of Quincy in population and wealth. In the year 1835 she contained about seven hundred inhabitants, with the following establishments, professional men, &c.:

10 stores, 1 pork merchant, 1 bonnet store, 3 cabinet shops, 3 cooper shops, 5 carpenter shops, 2 wagon makers, 3 brick makers, 4 tailors, 2 butchers, 1 silversmith, 1 chair maker, 6 physicians, 1 U. S. land office, 2 saw mills, 1 wool carding machine, 2 drug stores, 2 bakeries, 1 coach maker, 4 saddlers, 3 plasterers, 2 boot and shoe makers, 3 blacksmiths, 1 wheelwright, 6 lawyers, 1 printing office, 1 land agency, 1 steam flour mill, 3 taverns, 1 gunsmith.

Up to this year a large portion of the bacon and flour for home consumption had been imported, but from that date until the present, large and annually increasing amounts have been exported. The value of these exportations from July, 1834, to July, 1835, amounted to $40,000.

In 1837, the population had increased to 1,653, and produce was shipped as follows : Pork $85,000, Flour $19,500, Wheat, $8,000 worth.

Our space will not admit of a detailed enumeration of the advancement from year to year. Passing over the interval between 1838 and 1841, we find that the population in the latter year amounted to 2,686, and that the sale of merchandise of all sorts footed up to $329,800. Shipments of produce were as follows:— Wheat, 275,000 bushels, Corn, 95,000 bushels, Oats, 50,000 bushels, and during the same year 12,000 hogs were packed.

In 1849 the population had increased to 5,500, and there were in the city

26 retail variety stores, 2 hardware stores, 2 book stores, 3 drug stores, 2 foundries, 3 machine shops, 3 printing offices, 2 hotels, 9 physicians, 13 churches, 5 private schools, 5 dry goods stores, 10 ware houses, 4 steam flour mills, 2 steam saw mills, 7 pork houses, 4 lumber yards, 5 brick yards, 15 lawyers, 2 public schools."

Having thus only prefaced the early history of Quincy, we will in proper order enlarge upon the important events transpiring during the various stages of her progress, and give them due prominence.

MANUFACTURING AND COMMERCIAL INTERESTS OF QUINCY.

In most instances the best means of judging of the advantages of any locality, is by the extent of its commerce and manufactures. Occasionally we find this rule a poor one to apply, as we meet with cities and towns, which without any real advantages as commercial or manufacturing points, bloom into a sort of mushroom prosperity, and exist for a time with the same apparent indications of stability put forth by cities of a more substantial and permanent growth. But there has been no sudden or unaccountable growth of Quincy. From the first every step of its advance has been steady and unfaltering.

Admirably located on the high and healthy bluffs of the Mississippi river, 160 miles above St. Louis, and almost immediately at the foot of the "rapids," with a vast territory in Illinois, Missouri and Iowa, and the country farther west tributary to her, it required no prophetic eye to discern her future. Now the base of supplies for the vast regions above named, the wheels of commerce roll on with wondrous velocity to meet the constant demands for goods of all kinds. However the commercial success of Quincy was guaranteed at the outset by the surroundings of which she was the center. The fertility of the soil of the great "Prairie State," as well as the rich farming sections of Missouri adjacent to us, insured Quincy a large measure of prosperity without recourse to the other advantages that have made that prosperity loom up into such grand proportions in the past few years.

But the great problem, upon the solution of which depended more than all else the future of our city has been solved by the establishment and successful operation of the extensive mills, factories &c., that make up our manufacturing interests. Although we had much to expect from the ordinary mutations of commerce, it was hardly to be expected, even with our excellent location and surroundings, that we could build up an important city without drawing upon other resources. It is self-evident then that the key note of our greatest and most permanent prosperity was sounded when the sagacious men of the city determined to make this not only a commercial stronghold, but also an important manufacturing center. That resolve was carried out in good faith, and the days of experimenting with manufactures here gave way to the period when each year adds numerous extensive establishments to those that already tower up in every part of the city. Colossal tobacco factories, mammoth foundries, stately mills, extensive machine shops, planing and saw mills, boiler shops, and commodious edifices devoted to every department of manufacture are met with through the city. The busy hum of industry and enterprise is heard on all sides; and at evening the operatives and sons of toil from these establishments throng through our streets in hundreds, wending their way homeward after a day of labor.

That Quincy has many advantages as a manufacturing site over other western cities those who will give the subject proper consideration will be convinced. Although the enterprise started about a year ago, which promised to discover and develop inexhaustible coal mines in the very heart of the city, has not met with the success it was hoped would attend it, we still have vast coal mines connected with us by railroad, and are abundantly supplied by enterprising companies who furnish coal of excellent quality and at lower rates than is paid for the same by Chicago manufacturers and consumers. Should we succeed in finding coal in or near the city limits as many anticipate, the saving of cost of transportation would give our manufacturers still another advantage, and would give such an impetus to manufactures as would speedily place us in rivalry with Troy, Pittsburg, and other points, and soon swell our population to 100,000.

Besides having abundance of coal at fair rates we have an almost inexhaustible supply of wood for fuel in the vast forests on both sides of the river adjacent to the city. Here too, hard timber is obtained at a comparatively trifling expense, and saw mills convert it into lumber for use by the manufacturing establishments of the city.

Pine lumber from the great lumber districts of Wisconsin is brought here annually, and a supply equal to the necessities of the city is kept constantly on hand by our dealers.

Notwithstanding that most of our buildings are brick edifices the amount of lumber used here annually is enormous. When we consider however that over 500 buildings were erected in Quincy during the year 1868, it is not surprising. The amount of lumber shipped from here annually is also very large, and with the completion of the three new railroads now organized, and preparing for work, Quincy is destined to become an important lumber mart.

With the completion of these railroads comes as a matter of course, a large influx of laborers, mechanics and business men to swell our population and increase the local demand. Many too will be attracted here by the beauty and healthfulness of location, the comparatively small expense of living, the rare educational advantages offered, and the guarantee of liberal remuneration for labor in every field.

The position of Quincy upon the Mississippi River enables her readily to import the raw material which goes to supply her manufactories. In addition to this great natural advantage which affords cheap and reliable means during three-fourths of the year, for the distribution abroad of manufactured articles, as well as for the reception of materials, railroads are projected or built to the north, south, east and west, which when completed, which will be in a very short time, will prove an inestimable advantage to her manufacturing interest. On the west lies a country of unsurpassed fertility, of great extent, and rich in mineral resources, that must become tributary to her, if her citizens continue to push forward her railroad enterprises in this direction with the energy heretofore displayed, and she will thus be put in possession not only of a large and profitable trade, but of a plentiful supply of the products necessary to feed her work shops and factories.— Of these roads we propose to speak more in detail in a subsequent portion of this work. They are too important to pass over with a cursory remark, and are of vital interest to Quincy, not only as they relate to her manufacturing and commercial character, but in connection with every other department of social and industrial advancement. The facts which have been briefly stated, are a few of the peculiarities of position which enables Quincy to manufacture with such cheapness as to compete successfully in their own fields with such cities as Pittsburg, Cincinnati and St. Louis, each of which she is gradually supplanting in places heretofore dependent upon them for their supplies. They are sufficient to establish that her resources as a manufacturing city are unexcelled, so far as facilities for production are concerned. With regard to means of distribution she is equally fortunate. When we speak of her commercial facilities this will be apparent, for the same circumstances which favor the distribution of her wares, conduce to render her commerce extensive and valuable.

Under the head of "Railroads" and "River Commerce," we shall have occasion to note many items that argue the advantages of Quincy as a commercial and manufacturing center, and argue a future for her brighter than the anticipations of her most sanguine friends.

MERCANTILE AND MANUFACTURING INTERESTS.

In detailing the operations in the various mercantile and manufacturing departments of Quincy, we have used our utmost endeavors to obtain accurate figures and statements with a view to present our city in its proper light, as well to the capitalist as to the producing and laboring classes. In some cases we have been unable to procure as full statistics as we had hoped for, owing to the objections of many business men to making their operations and transactions public. With our leading manufacturing and business firms no such objection has been raised, and we give a full and accurate report of the business of the year, which will in most instances be found less than an average of their annual operations. The cause of the discrepancy this year in many departments of trade and manufacture as compared with previous years is not that we have been less enterprising or more sorely afflicted with "hard times" than other localities, but may be readily traced to the general depression of business throughout the country the present year.

In many departments of trade however, business has increased rather than decreased, and our leading manufacturing interests have prospered to a degree that far exceeded the anticipations of the most sanguine.

The year just closing has added a number of colossal establishments to the mercantile interests of Quincy, and also several extensive manufacturing houses.— While other points have felt the severity of the times, there has been comparatively little complaint here, and our business men have done handsomely. This is the more gratifying when it is understood that on all sides it is conceded business must vastly increase from this time forward, and even in a greater ratio than in years past. Our hopes in this respect are not ill-founded, for with the completion of the four railroads now projected and guaranteed, Quincy must rapidly advance in population, wealth, and commercial importance. The best indication of our prospects however, is to be found in the daily augmentation of our population, and the fact that shrewd business men from all sections of the country are arriving here and establishing themselves in the various departments of trade. That they find inducements here not offered by any city of like size in the west, all who have visited Quincy and posted themselves in regard to her advantages and resources will readily admit. To those who have never troubled themselves to inquire into the present position and future prospects of our city, we submit the facts and figures contained in this little volume as evidence of our commercial, manufacturing, and social status, confident that the exhibit will not be even approximated by any city of 40,000 inhabitants in the west.

MANUFACTURES.

FLOUR.

To no department of her manufactures is Quincy more largely indebted for the enviable reputation she has achieved as a manufacturing center, than to her milling interests. The manufacture of flour was commenced early in her history, and the embryo "grist mill" established in 1824, by a shrewd yankee named Dr. Baker, has grown to be one of the most important manufacturing interests centered here.

In this department a vast amount of capital is employed, and the annual product of our milling establishments is large. But not alone we have we a reputation for the *quantity* of flour annually produced here, but the *quality* is such that it ranks with the famous brands of the country. Everywhere the demand for it is greater than the supply, and in Liverpool and other European markets it is known almost as well as in our home markets. But the success that has crowned our manufactures in this line is not surprising or unaccountable. Besides the vast capital engaged in building up this interest, and bringing it to its present pre-eminent position among the great flour marts of this country, the time, talent and labor of many of our most enterprising citizens has been devoted to the same work for a score or more years. The costly and extensive establishments employed in the manufacture of flour that tower up in Quincy now, were not all built in a day.— When Osborn, and Bagby and others who have been largely instrumental in making Quincy a great flour mart commenced that arduous work, they operated in no such noble structures as the present "Eagle," "Tellico," or "Castle" mills, but were confined to more modest and less capacious establishments. However, with such men, no matter how humble their beginning, success was only a question of time. Ripe with sagacity, full of energy, and alive with enterprise, each year witnessed some new improvement, some needed addition to their establishments, until almost unperceived, success was achieved, and they found themselves at the head of colossal mills, not surpassed by those of the great cities of the east. There was no longer any question as to the feasibility of profitably manufacturing flour in Quincy, and many embarked in the enterprise. We have now ten establishments engaged in its manufacture, most of them model concerns, with all the improvements which experience has recommended. Several of these mills, the Eagle, Castle, Tellico, City, &c., have a capacity of 300 barrels per day, and all of these are almost constantly kept running.

A magnificent area of wheat country surrounds Quincy, and the quality of the wheat raised is of the very best. Much excellent wheat is also brought here annually from Minnesota and Wisconsin by the river at a moderate cost of transportation, and is converted into flour by our mills.

The demand for Quincy flour comes from all quarters,

and is always in excess of the supply, and while much of it in the transmutations of commerce finds its way to the seaboard and across the Atlantic, other large quantities of it go westward over the plains and to the Rocky Mountains. In Salt Lake City this flour is largely consumed, and is reported to give better satisfaction than any that is offered to the saints and prophets of that remarkable place.

The manufacture of flour is now carried on by the following firms, who have met with merited success.— They are among the most energetic and enterprising of our citizens, and the future cannot but add to their prosperity and success.

NAME OF MILLS.	FIRM.	CAPACITY PER DAY.
Eagle Mills	W. H. Osborn & Co.,	350 barrels.
Castle Mills	Bagby & Wood,	300 "
Tellico Mills	Dick Bros.,	350 "
City Mills	C. E. Whitmore	300 "
Star Mills	Wheeler & Cruttenden,	100 "
Quincy Mills	Monning Bros.,	100 "
City Springs Mills	W. Hunerwadel,	100 "
Centre Mills,	Allen & Whyers,	300 "
Farmers' Mills	Crockett & Mason	150 "
Royal Mills	Osborn & Naylor,	

The past year there has been less done by our mills than any season for ten years previous, and we therefore refrain from publication of the year's operations, as it would not be anything like a fair average. They have however given employment to 130 hands, and have done a profitable business. The capital invested is about $400,000.

Ex-Gov. JOHN WOOD, "Father of Quincy."

In the sketch we are about to give of Ex-Governor John Wood, who is appropriately called the "Father of Quincy," we are well aware that we will not do full justice to that venerable citizen, to whom more than any other Quincy is indebted for all she is and expects to be. But while we may not fill the measure of expectation in the minds of our readers, it will require little effort to lay before them a sketch replete with interesting facts and remarkable events in the life of one, around whose name cluster so many glorious recollections and memorable associations. Although we know that we could do him no greater displeasure than publish his virtues and great deeds to the world, it is a duty we owe our readers who venerate and love the man, to award a prominent place in this work to the founder, friend, and "Father of Quincy."

Few men have passed through a more eventful career than the Hon. John Wood. Born in 1795, in the State of New York, he had scarcely passed the age of maturity, when we find him tracking across the great wilds of the north-west to the sparsely settled Valley of the Mississippi. In the fall of 1821, he arrived in the neigborhood of the now populous City of Quincy, with two companions, one of whom owned some land in the vicinity. At once impressed with the beauty of the spot, and its admirable geographical position, he resolved, in his own words, to "settle here for life."— The succeeding fall he returned, and erected the first house within the present bounds of Quincy. In the spring following, Mr. Wood was joined by a family from New York, and shortly after Willard Keyes and John Droullard, a Frenchman, were added to the little settlement. At that time there was no white settlement within sixty miles of Quincy on the south, or forty on the north.

In 1825 through the efforts of John Wood, the county of Adams was organized, and the little settlement was fixed upon as the County Seat, and christened in honor of the President, "Quincy."

Thus early John Wood manifested an untiring zeal for the advancement and prosperity of the young settlement, and from that time until now, his zeal for the improvement and success of Quincy, has not abated the least.

In the spring of 1844, John Wood was elected Mayor of the city, and so efficiently and faithfully did he serve the city in that position, that he was elected for three successive terms following. In 1852, he was again called to the helm of city affairs, and in 1853 was re-elected. Three years having elapsed he was again called by the people of Quincy to the mayoralty, and administered the affairs of the city with the same success and satisfaction for which he was proverbial.

But the reputation of John Wood was not confined to Quincy alone, for throughout the State he was recognized as one of its greatest and best citizens. Being an ardent Whig in 1856, he was nominated on the ticket with Gov. Bissell, for Lieutenant Governor, and elected. The former dying, the duties of Governor devolved upon the latter, and he performed them with signal ability.

At the outbreak of the war in 1861, Gov. Wood being an ardent advocate of the cause of the Union, was appointed Quarter Master General of the State of Illinois. His devotion to the soldiers of Illinois, and his efforts to alleviate their sufferings on the field and in the hospitals of the country, are a part of the records of Illinois patriotism.

But, unimpeachable as has been the public life of Gov. Wood, his private life has been pregnant with noble deeds and generous works that are not paled by his most distinguished services in behalf of the city, state, or nation.

Eminent for his great qualities of head and heart, his munificent donations to the charitable institutions of Quincy, and his liberal encouragement of every worthy enterprise, are household words in the city.

Advanced to the ripe old age of 74, with a constitution still vigorous and active, Gov. Wood has the proud privilege of witnessing the growth in beauty, wealth and dignity of the city that he, with wondrous sagacity, planted nearly fifty-eight years ago. A man of sterling integrity, and a radical advocate of right, Gov. Wood is kind and affable in his disposition, and in his declining years enjoys the friendship and veneration of all who know him.

TOBACCO MANUFACTORIES.

Among the most prominent features in the manufacturing list is that of Tobacco. Four large establishments are at present in active operation, employing an actual capital of $345,000, with gross sales exceeding $1,300,000, as well as giving constant employment to 560 hands. The tobacco manufactured in these estabments reaches every market in the Union, commanding the highest prices, owing to the admirable adaptation of this climate to that particular business, as well as the superior business qualifications of the proprietors, whose thorough knowledge of the business has been gained by long experience and close application, allowing no improvement to escape them, regardless of trouble or expense, and hence their great success.— Hundreds of little boys and girls find constant employment in these establishments, thus enabling them to earn not only a living for themselves, but also to furnish food and raiment for their widowed mothers and smaller brothers and sisters, who would otherwise be thrown upon the cold charities of the public, and would of necessity suffer not only for food, but also from the chilly blasts of winter.

No less than two of these establishments have agents in the Virginia, Tennessee and Kentucky tobacco markets, whose business it is to purchase the very best of tobacco sold in these markets. Therefore they are enabled to supply their customers with the very best brands that can be found in any market in the Union.

The following are the factories now in operation and the names of firms operating the same.

FACTORY.	FIRM.
Eclipse Tobacco Works	J. R. Harris & Co.
Empire Tobacco Works	Harris, Beebe & Co.
Liberty Tobacco Works	Binkert Bros. & Ware.
Gem City Tobacco Works	Thos. H. Collins & Co.
National Tobacco Works	H. E. Jansen & Co.

Besides the above named, which are devoted exclusively to the manufacture of plug tobacco, we have in our city two factories engaged in manufacturing smoking tobacco.

HON. THOS. JASPER, VICE PRES. 1ST NAT. BANK.

OR "MEN OF MARK" IN QUINCY.

Few of the prominent business men of Quincy have had so uninterrupted a career of prosperity as the subject of this sketch.

Hon. Thomas Jasper is a native of the State of Kentucky, and came to Quincy from that State in 1837, being then a young man, just starting in life. Like most of the now "solid men" of our city, Mr Jasper's capital on his arrival in Quincy consisted of a vigorous constitution, a brave heart and a determined spirit, and with these he began the conflict of life. Shortly after locating here he was elected constable, and filled that position until 1840, when he was elected sheriff of Adams county. At the expiration of his term of office as sheriff, he invested what funds he had accumulated in a stock of groceries, and opened a store. For ten years he devoted himself to merchandising, and then retiring from mercantile business, bought an interest in the distillery on the Bay, known as "King's." On the death of Mr. King, Mr. Jasper succeeded to the ownership and management of the entire business, and as was invariably the case, with whatever he was connected, it yielded handsome profits.

In 1860, Mr. Jasper was elected Mayor of Quincy, and in 1868 was chosen as one of the representatives in the State Legislature from Adams County. We have above traced briefly some of the steps in his life in Quincy, but much more remains to be said that might be better said by an abler pen. Through his entire career as officer, merchant, manufacturer, mayor or legislator, he was ever active and faithful, and retained the confidence of the entire community. Now one of the wealthiest of our citizens, he is indebted alone to his own exertions for what he possesses, and none contribute with a more liberal hand to any enterprise that promises to improve the status of Quincy, socially or otherwise. An earnest advocate of railroads, his time and means have been liberally given to forward them, and for the past few months it is well known that he has worked with a zeal surpassed by none in behalf of the proposed new roads. One of the founders of the Quincy Savings Bank, now the First National, he is at present Vice President of that solid institution.

In personal appearance Mr. Jasper presents a fine type of the substantial business man. With an open inviting countenance, a massive forehead and a piercing eye, his face indicates the man—frank, generous and determined, a genial gentleman, an irreproachable citizen, a steadfast friend, such is the Hon. Thomas Jasper, than whom Quincy boasts no better man.

MACHINE SHOPS.

It was to be expected that in a city devoted so largely to manufactures as Quincy, there would be establishments for turning out the machinery and implements demanded in every branch of manufactures. That expectation has however been more than realized, for not only have we extensive machine shops, but we have also mechanics, whose skill and genius have made them famous wherever steam is employed as a motive power, or wherever the steam engine is found. More than this, our machine shops are now and have been for years shipping to all parts of the west their machines and implements. Nor are we to wonder at the demand for Quincy work in this line. All the establishments devoted to this branch of manufactures are models in every respect, provided with every facility and improvement, and managed by master mechanics. But while our machine shops have performed a noble part in building up our city and in supplying localities all thro' the west with the means of forwarding their development and growth, they have not rested there. Not content to shape and build that which the minds of others had conceived, Quincy genius has itself been active in the field of invention, and from our dusky workshops have sprung inventions and improvements in mechanism to which humanity is indebted for their time, labor and life saving character.

The celebrated "Automaton Steam Governor," patented by Robert W. Gardner, Esq., of this city, and which is used all over the continent, may be cited as no ordinary achievement in mechanism.

In the same connection may be mentioned the famous "Iron Barge" for transporting grain in bulk, invented by John Williams, Esq., of Quincy, and which was awarded the first prize by the committee of old and experienced shippers and steamboat men at the great St. Louis fair of 1868, a score or more contestants being present,

So well is the reputation of our machine shops established that they are kept constantly busy with large forces of men, supplying the steady and increasing demand for work in their line. This demand comes from almost every section of the states west of us, and even Chicago and St. Louis draw on Quincy for steam engines, &c., occasionally. All work in this department is turned out in the best possible style, and will compare in strength, durability, and finish with any from the oldest and best establishments of the east,

At present the following firms are engaged in manufacturing machinery and doing a general machine business:—John Williams & Co., Gardner & Robertson, S. G. Tyler, M. T. Greenleaf, Worrell, Bert & Co., W. Hagen, J. Schaffner, P. Schwebel. These establishments employ constantly about 360 hands, and do a business of $1,050,000 a year. The capital invested in this branch of manufactures is $240,000.

FOUNDRIES.

We have in our city several extensive foundries, but most of them are connected with machine shops, and properly come under that head. Others are separate and distinct, and all are managed by experienced and skillful mechanics. They are prepared to turn out all classes of work in iron and brass, and in the best possible style. In this line improvement has been more marked than in perhaps any branch of manufactures, and there is scarcely any article or implement used in mechanism that cannot be obtained here. Brass molding is now extensively carried on at these establishments, and is executed in a high order of workmanship and finish.

It is only within a few years that our mechanics have attempted work of this class, but they have been so successful in the undertaking that they have enlarged their facilities, and gone into it on an extensive scale. They have already built up a large trade, and we have now in successful operation an extensive establishment for the sale of machinist's supplies, iron and brass finishings, &c. Here, everything needed in the largest manufacturing establishment can be had at more advantageous rates than in larger cities, and the prospect is fair to make Quincy the base of supplies for goods in this line of a vast section of the west.

The following firms are now carrying on foundries, but as much of the products of their establishments has been estimated under the head of Machine Shops, it is not deemed necessary to restate the amount of work turned out by them:—John Williams & Co.; M. T. Greenleaf; Smith, Hayner & Co.; Worrell, Bert & Co.; E. Sien; P. Lally.

These firms employ a large number of hands, most of whom have also been included in the estimate of those engaged in the manufacture of machinery.

STOVES.

In the manufacture of Stoves and Hollow Ware Quincy ranks second to no city west of Pittsburg for the amount of work annually turned out. The establishments devoted to this branch of manufactures are built on an extensive scale, and are provided with all the improvements and appurtenances that long years of skillful management have suggested as most desirable. The best mechanics that the country affords are employed here, and receive handsome wages for their labor.

The vast territory that seeks Quincy for supplies in this line has necessitated a yearly increase in the amount of stoves manufactured, and our foundries have repeatedly enlarged their facilities for supplying this demand. We have now one of the largest stove foundries in the Union, and all in operation here employ large forces of hands. The success that has attended our manufacturers in this department is more than flattering, and the future promises even brighter results than have yet been achieved. Trade continues to enlarge annually and stoves from this market are now shipped to all points in the Mississippi Valley and in the states and territories west. Wherever they have been introduced, satisfaction is guaranteed, and a foothold once gained, a permanent trade is established.

Quincy owes much to the enterprising proprietors and managers of these extensive establishments, as they have been vastly beneficial to her, and have been second to no other interest in building up our city, and increasing its wealth and power. Besides the large amount annually paid out to mechanics, and thus distributed through the channels of commerce, this branch of manufactures has added material wealth to Quincy in the colossal establishments erected by the enterprising men engaged in it. Few even of our own citizens have an idea of the extent of this business, and we therefore give some items of information below.

This year the stove foundries of our city employed 314 hands and manufactured 36,400 stoves, which at an average of $13 a piece amounts to $473,200. The following are the firms now engaged in this branch of manufactures :—Comstock, Castle & Co.; Bonnet & Duffy ; Excelsior Works, (co-operative,) ; Thomas White.

HON. WILLIAM A. RICHARDSON,
OR "MEN OF MARK" IN QUINCY.

Quincy has had a large share in shaping the destinies and administering the affairs of the nation, and many of her citizens have rendered eminent service in her councils of state. Of these none have had so extended and eventful a career as the Hon. Wm. A. Richardson.

Born in Kentucky in 1811, he came to Illinois in 1831, and thus early commenced the practice of law, in Shelby County, although not quite out of his teens. His success at the bar was so marked that in 1834 the Legislature elected him to the responsible position of State's Attorney. This position he resigned in 1836, on his election to the Legislature from Schuyler County. In 1838 he was again sent by his constituents to the Legislature, this time as a member of the Senate, where he served four years. Two years having expired he was a second time elected to the House of Representatives, and upon its organization was elected speaker. The same year he was one of the Presidential Electors on the Democratic ticket.

On the breaking out of the war with Mexico Mr. Richardson, although just at the spring-tide of political preferment, with the honors and emoluments of office within his grasp, resolved to espouse the cause of his country on the field of strife. Raising a company, he at once went to the front and did noble service. Devoted to his men, a brave and humane officer, on the field of Buena Vista he was for gallant conduct promoted to the position of Lieutenant Colonel by the unanimous voice of his regiment.

Returning home with the laurels of the field, exalted honors awaited him, and he was promptly elected to Congress to fill the vacancy occasioned by the resignation of Judge Douglas. Re-elected in 1848, and for three successive terms immediately following, Col. Richardson continued in Congress until 1856, and was a recognized leader of his party in that body. On his retirement from Congress, he was nominated by the Democracy of Illinois for Governor, but was defeated by Gov. Bissell, the majority of the latter being only 3000.

The administration of President Buchanan coming into power, he was in 1857, appointed by the President Governor of the then territory of Nebraska. This position however he retained only one year, when he again returned to Quincy. Here in 1860 he again received the nomination, and was again elected to Congress where he served until 1863, when he resigned to accept a seat in the United States Senate to which he had been elected to fill the vacancy occasioned by the death of the lamented Douglas. The political complexion of the State and Nation having undergone a great change, and the Republican party being in the ascendant in both, at the expiration of his term in the Senate, Col. Richardson sought the retirement of his home in Quincy.

Although this remarkable man has passed through the eventful and distinguished career here briefly sketched, he is still vigorous in mind and body, and is destined to yet do valuable service in the interests of the nation. A man of warm and generous impulses, of powerful intellect and bold ideas, Col. Richardson has at all times wielded a giant influence with the masses, and has found few equals as a stump orator, while in the great councils of his party his native eloquence has been no less potent. Few men have had more devoted followers in the arena of politics; and of all the great men with whom he has mingled, none have been more steadfast to principle and party than the Hon. Wm. A. Richardson.

BREWERIES.

With the large German element of Quincy it was not unnatural to suppose there would be an active demand for beer. Such is the fact, but it is a question whether the Germans, or other nationalities of Quincy consume the most. One fact is apparent, that all classes of our citizens enjoy this beverage as heartily as those of Teutonic extraction. But as the drink is decidedly, and by common consent German, Quincy with almost half its population German, could not well exist without a fair share of breweries for the manufacture of the same.— We have these then in abundance, and all are model establishments, one or two of them not being second to any in the west, in capacity and facilities for making beer. In quality Quincy beer ranks with the best article manufactured, and hence the great and growing demand from abroad. All points on the railroads diverging from here, and also for a considerable distance up and down the Mississippi obtain their supplies from our breweries, and as far west as St. Joseph and Leavenworth the foaming beverage from Quincy establishments is sold. Each year witnesses an increase in the demand, and a consequent increase of the supply. Several of our breweries have been compelled to add to their capacity annually for several years, so constantly has their trade augmented. The manufacturers in this line need make no exertion whatever to dispose of their beer, as almost invariably towards the close of the season they are compelled to husband their supply in order to fill their orders. This trade moreover is destined to be permanent, for the men engaged in the business are of the energetic and enterprising type, who will not fail to maintain the reputation they have already established for the product of their breweries.

The following are the firms now engaged in this branch of manufacture.

Dick Bros.; Eber & Hoering; C. Fischer; A. L. Luther; J. Luther & Co.; Ruff Bros. & Co.; H. Rupp.

These employ an aggregate capital of $335,000, and manufacture annually 207,000 kegs of beer. One hundred and seventy hands also find employment in these establishments.

PAPER.

One of the youngest enterprises in Quincy is the manufacture of paper, which is carried on successfully. Within a few years two extensive factories have been erected at an enormous expenditure of money, and fitted up with the best machinery and equipments to be had in the country. These factories have facilities for manufacturing all qualities of straw, wrapping and newspaper, and have, in the short time they have been in operation built up a splendid trade. Only one is now in operation, although the other is ready to commence running at any time. In this trade our manufacturers find it an easy matter to compete with eastern houses, as they manufacture equally as good paper, and can supply points at the west at more advantageous rates. The past year has not been an active one in this branch, but with a few seasons of successful work, our mills will establish a reputation for the products of their establishments that will attract the trade to Quincy, and make it a leading paper mart. There is every reason why it should be, as material and labor are obtained here cheaper than at rival points, and the facilities for manufacturing on the river bank are such as to induce others to embark in the enterprise. One thing alone is necessary to make the manufacture of paper profitable, and that is capital sufficient to run a mill steadily.

The two mills now located here are model ones in every respect, and are owned and managed by men of business skill and enterprise. The firms are II. A. Geise & Son, and Woodruff & Boyd. At present, one of these mills being idle, no estimate of the amount of annual work done by them can be obtained.

Hon. O. H. BROWNING,
OR "MEN OF MARK" IN QUINCY.

A history of the bar of Quincy would form an interesting volume, and to do full justice to the eminent men whose achievements in jurisprudence have shed lustre upon that distinguished body, would be a work worthy the most gifted pen in the land. Here many of the ablest and most erudite lawyers of Illinois won their first laurels, and began the conflict of life in which they have won renown, reflecting credit and honor alike upon themselves and their chosen state.

Pre-eminent among these chieftains of the bar whose fame has become national stands Hon. O. H. Browning, the subject of this sketch. As early as 1831 Mr. Browning left his native state, Kentucky, and armed with his license, located in Quincy as a member of the bar. With a clear mind, full of industry and energy, he was not slow in merging into prominence, even among the great intellects who were accustomed to make the tour of this circuit—which then embraced Quincy, Chicago, Galena, &c. His reputation once established, a lucrative practice rewarded his fidelity and industry, and political honors sought him.

In August, 1836, he was elected to the Senate of Illinois, and served four years in that body. About this time Nehemiah Bushnell, his present law partner, arrived in Quincy, and in 1837 the law partnership was formed, which has continued 32 years, and still exists. In 1842 Mr. Browning was again elected to the State Legislature, serving two years as a member of the House. He however allowed nothing to divert his attention from his law practice, but devoted himself assiduously to the interests of his clients. With the intermission of making unsuccessful canvasses, as the Whig candidate for Congress, Mr. Browning, figured but little in the political arena from 1844 to 1861.

Upon the death of Judge Douglas, Governor Yates selected Mr. Browning as the fittest person to succeed that lamented statesman in the Senate of the United States. Retiring from the Senate he opened a law office at the National Capital, associating himself with Senator Cowan of Pennsylvania. He continued there until 1866, when President Johnson reorganizing his Cabinet, called Mr. Browning to the responsible position of Secretary of the Interior. This position he retained until the close of Mr. Johnson's term, administering its voluminous affairs with signal success. Returning home, Mr. Browning had determined on a period of retirement and rest, after the arduous labors devolving on him while a Cabinet Officer, but his old friends and fellow citizens again made a requisition upon his time and talent by electing him a member of the Constitutional Convention of Illinois.

Thus briefly we have noted some of the events in the life of one of the distinguished men of the country.—Quincy may well be proud of so eminent a citizen, who having filled the most exalted stations in the gift of the State and Nation retires the acknowledged peer of the greatest statesman of his time.

THE ORPHANS.

THEIR CARE AND EDUCATION—WOODLAND HOME—ST. ALOYSIUS ASYLUM.

In matters of public enterprise and public charity the citizens of Quincy have been as liberal as in private affairs. Nothing that has been introduced to the notice of our citizens that directly or indirectly promised to advance the interests of the city but what has received their cordial encouragement and support, and in like manner they have with Christian liberality, responded to the calls of charity.

Every city that has attained the size and importance of our own, finds within its borders numbers of young and helpless children who, without parents or friends, are obliged to seek protection and assistance at the hands of the public. This being the case, our citizens, with a liberality proverbial in them, several years ago turned their attention to the cause of the orphans.

ST. ALOYSIUS SOCIETY.

Something over eleven years ago a society was formed among the members of ehe German Catholic Church in this city, and by an act of the Legislature it was incorporated under the name of St. Aloysius Orphan Society. The society at once set to work with a zeal peculiar to the people, and after accumulating a large fund from annual picnics and entertainments, two years ago began the erection of an Asylum devoted to the orphans of Quincy without regard to clime or creed. The building was speedily completed and the society at once engaged a band of Sisters belonging to the order of "Sisters of Notre Dame" to assume control of the same. They began their work four years ago, and since that time have devoted themselves to the good work of caring for and educating the orphans placed under their charge. The Asylum is located on the corner of Twentieth and Vine streets, is a plain but large and commodious structure, three stories high with a fine basement, and has a lot of 300 feet square surrounding it. It contains fourteen rooms which are respectively reception room, parlor, work rooms, play rooms, refectory, school room, chapel, dormitory, &c.

The reception room is neat and convenient,—the parlor is large and airy and the dormitories are spacious and well ventilated and are furnished with neat and comfortable single beds for the use of the orphans.

The work room is devoted, we may say, exclusively to the use of girls, and they are taught here the use of the needle, and also gain an insight into household affairs. The room is appropriately furnished. A school room, where they are given an ordinary English education, is an other interesting department of the asylum, and here the orphans, both boys and girls, are collected each day for intellectual training. The result is that when they leave the institution, even though they have no immediate friends, they are prepared to battle through life and hew out a destiny for themselves. A splended refectory is also a feature of the St. Aloysius Asylum, and here the little orphans are served with plain and substantial food, prepared by the good sisters. That they are are amply provided, no better evidence is needed than the hearty appearance presented by them as they circulate through the building.

Two dormitories are provided, one for the boys, the other for the girls. Tiers of single beds range through them, and as they are each surrounded with tidy curtains, they present a pleasant appearance. There is also a Chapel where the ceremonies of the Catholic church are daily held, and though orphans of every clime and creed are admitted to the asylum they are not obliged to profess the Catholic faith to receive its benefits, yet they are required to attend the services in the chapel each day in order that they may not interfere with the discipline of the establishment.

As we have said the asylum was erected by the St. Aloysious Orphan Society, but that society has been aided in its work of charity by the citizens of Quincy without regard to sect or nationality. Every one of our citizens have added their mite to the munificent sum expended by this society in the erection and maintainance of this institution that has been such a source of good in the community. The labor of conducting the establishment has devolved upon the Sisters in charge, who at present number seven, under the superiorship of Sister Mary Hypollita. These Sisters have devoted their lives to the work of protecting and educating the young and helpless, and are zealously giving their time and talents to the cause. Whatever may be the opinion of the people in regard to the sect and order to which they belong, the Sisters of Notre Dame deserve great praise for the self-sacrificing spirit they display in the cause of charity.

WOODLAND HOME.

Although we have devoted considerable space and time to the Sisters de Notre Dame and the Asylum under their control, still they have not been alone in the good work, nor is theirs the only one of the kind in our flourishing city. Woodland Home was incorporated by an act of the Legislature of Illinois, on the 14th of February, 1855.

At a meeting of the trustees of "Woodland Home for the Orphans and Friendless," held at the First Congregational Church, Quincy, Illinois, at 8 o'clock P. M., on the 1st day of July, 1859:

Present—John Wood, Willard Keyes, Frederick Collins, Joel Rice, Hiram Rogers, Newton Flagg, Elijah Gove, John Wheeler, and Orville H. Browning.

On motion, Hon. John Wood was called to the chair, and O. H. Browning appointed Secretary.

Being thus organized, a constitution for the government of said corporation was unanimously adopted.

Deciding afterwards to make the care of orphans and friendless women a speciality, they changed the name in 1855, to the Woodland Home for Orphans and Friendless Women.

From that time to this, regular meetings have been held, and each month one lady has devoted herself to the care and interests of the Home. A very efficient corps of ladies has managed the charities of the Society. Its operations have been carried on amid great vicisitudes and discouragement. For years they had no building for a Home, and boarded their children in families where kind people could be found to care for and look after the moral and physical wants of the little ones.

Many times the hindrances in their path seemed insurmountable, but a way was always made for their feet when the time came to go forward. Now, after nearly sixteen years of arduous labor, they wish to testify to the care of God, and the sympathy and aid of the community. Though often brought very low, the barrel of meal was never quite wasted, and the garment has always been supplied which was needed to secure comfort or covering. It was, and still is the intention of the Society, to erect on the five acre lot purchased of Hon. John Wood for this purpose, suitable buildings for the Woodland Home. Hiram Rogers, Esq., recently deceased, generously bestowed $5,000 to the Society, and they have been repeatedly placed under obligations for evidences of liberality towards the Home.

Unable at present to erect such buildings as they deemed adequate to the wants of the Society and worthy of Quincy, they purchased in 1867 the residence of the late George Brown, situated on Fifth and Washington streets, at a cost of $15,500. Here there is a large, commodious and well ventilated building, with 14 rooms and a yard 200 feet square.

The Society has at all times had more or less orphans and helpless friendless persons under its control. These children are all educated, and their moral training is well provided for. Each Sabbath they attend the Congregational Sabbath School, and there are early imbued with the truths of religion.

These two institutions are and should be the pride of our citizens as they are living monuments to our christian enterprise. They are the trumpets that speak the fame of a people, who out of the abundance of their possessions give to the friendless and destitute orphans, and who, in building here upon the banks of the mighty Mississippi a great city, have not forgotten the teachings of religion and humanity,

HON. MAITLAND BOON,

OR "MEN OF MARK IN QUINCY."

Though one of the youngest of those whose names appear in this work on account of their efforts in behalf of Quincy and Quincy enterprises, the subject of this sketch stands second to none as a citizen of enterprise, energy, and public spirit.

Maitland Boon was born in Watertown, New York, in 1834, and there, after leaving college began his experience in business. He first entered a drug house, and devoted himself to that business for two years, when an opportunity offering he accepted the position of discount clerk in the Union Bank of Watertown.—His time in this position was however brief, and at the expiration of two years he was called by the management of the bank to the important and responsible position of cashier. This position Mr. Boon filled with credit to himself and profit to the institution, until 1856, when he decided to cast his fortunes with the growing west. It was in this year that he came to Quincy and located. Tendered the position of cashier of the Bank of Quincy, he accepted, and during his connection with the same managed its affairs with a judgment and ability that stamped him as an able financier. Retiring from the bank, Mr. Boon established himself in the saddlery and harness business, conducting one of the most extensive manufactories of this kind in the west. During the war he did a mammoth business in the manufacture of army equipments, filling large contracts for the government. In 1865 the office of mayor of Quincy becoming vacant, Mr. Boon, then an alderman from the second ward, was appointed to that position. So ably did he fulfill the important trust confided to him, and so satisfactorily discharge its duties that in the following spring he was elected by an overwhelming majority to the mayorality. The last year he officiated as executive of the city with even greater success than the first, and won enthusiastic encomiums from citizens of both parties for his admirable management of city affairs.

Although a large share of his attention while mayor was unavoidably absorbed by city matters, Mr. Boon did not during that period neglect his own affairs, but did an extensive business in the manufacture and sale of harness, saddles, &c. Soon after the expiration of his term of office, Mr. Boon, feeling in common with many of the citizens of Quincy the necessity of having in our city a first-class hotel, obtained a lease of the famous Quincy House, then unoccupied, and after furnishing it in elegant style, and improving it in every department, opened it to the public. For two years he has managed this house in admirable style, and won golden laurels as a successful and popular landlord. Although but 35 years, of age Mr. Boon has had a varied career as a business man and financier. A man of warm and generous impulses, of a genial and social nature, Maitland Boon is also a man of untiring energy and enterprise, making at once the valuable citizen and popular gentleman.

DISTILLERIES.

Before the war several extensive distilleries were almost continually in operation and turned out annually immense quantities of highwines, besides feeding great numbers of cattle and hogs. Even after the war had commenced, and the revenue system had been introduced, two of these establishments continued to operate night and day, consuming vast quantities of corn, and employing a large number of hands. The operation of the revenue system, however, working disadvantageously to them, they were finally compelled to cease work, in order to save themselves. Dishonest manufacturers multiplied so rapidly throughout the country, and frauds upon the revenue were so extensive, that to manufacture highwines honestly, and at the same time make it profitable, was an impossibility. Our distilleries, that had been paying the government as high as $150,000 a month tax, therefore closed. Since the reduction of the taxes and the perfection of the revenue system, they have occasionally operated for a short time, but have not run steadily or to their full capacity. This is the more unfortunate at the present time, as it not only robs our farmers of a splendid market for their corn, but also throws a number of hands out of employment. One of the most important manufacturing interests of our city and one in which a vast amount of capital is invested, it has added large material wealth to Quincy.

Both of the firms now owning distilleries here are comprised of solid and enterprising citizens, who will not allow their establishments to remain idle long, when they can afford to operate them.

These firms are: Charles H. Curtis & Co., and Cramer & Brockschmidt. Very little work has been done this year, and we therefore make no estimate.

CARRIAGES.

This is another department of Quincy manufactures in which the superior skill and workmanship of our mechanics have won an enviable reputation for themselves and the city. It is but a few years ago that some of our shrewdest citizens then engaged in the manufacture of carriages, concluded to retire from it, feeling that it was next to impossible to compete in this branch with eastern cities, where the work had been, through long years of experience, brought to a high degree of perfection. Notwithstanding this, other indomitable spirits engaged in the enterprise, and followed it through years of experiment and uncertainty to the pinnacle of success. Now it is one of the important branches of our manufactures, and has done as much as any one thing to introduce Quincy favorably to the outside world. Wherever carriages bearing the brand of our factories are sold, and they are to be seen almost everywhere west of the Mississippi, and in the cities and towns adjacent to it, they are known for their strength, durability and high style of finish. This business has now become a marked success here, and carriages, buggies and vehicles from this market compete successfully with those from the famous factories of New Haven, Rochester, and Philadelphia. A large business is now also being done by our manufacturers in this line, in building coaches for the stage lines of the west, and also omnibusses. In this particular they have achieved splendid success, and orders have been received from localities far removed from us for vehicles of this kind. For enterprise and activity, as well as thorough business skill, our carriage manufacturers yield the palm to no city in the Union, and are destined to build up an extensive trade all through the west. At present they are doing a large business and are kept actively at work with large forces of mechanics. The firms now engaged in this branch are:—E. M. Miller & Co.; Hynes & Moore; Grotenhoff & Behrens; Kœnig & Weiler.

These employ 93 hands, and turn out annually $269,140 worth of work.

Hon. JAMES M. PITMAN,
OR "MEN OF MARK IN QUINCY."

Of all the leading men whose energy and ability have been active in building up the flourishing city of Quincy, and advancing its interests, it is fair to say none take rank before the Hon. James M. Pitman.

Born in the then territory of Missouri, in 1813, at the age of 22 he came to Quincy, and at once interested himself in not only carving out his own success, but also in forwarding our city commercially and socially. Obtaining an interest in a saw mill, he operated that for a time with decided success, and in 1844 had so commended himself to the voters of Adams County that he was elected Sheriff. So admirably did he perform the duties of the office the first two years that he was chosen by his constituents for a second term, and continued in the responsible position until 1848. On retiring from the office, he embarked in the lumber business, with Amos Green, Esq., as a partner. Success attended the firm, and in its career both members accumulated wealth with comparative rapidity.

In 1850 Mr. Pitman was elected as a representative to the Legislature, and in 1852 was returned to that body. While there he devoted himself assiduously to the interests of Quincy and Adams County, and by his industry secured much legislation that has been of vast advantage to Quincy. Among other items he obtained a charter for a Gas Company, a Mississippi River Bridge Company, and also the charter under which the great Chicago, Burlington & Quincy Railroad was built.

Scarcely had his labors in the councils of the State ended when he was called to the mayoralty of Quincy in 1854. Managing the affairs of the city with the same skill and success that had characterized his own private matters, he was re-elected in 1855, and retired with an enviable reputation for integrity and ability as an executive officer. Only a short period of relaxation followed his retirement from the municipal government of Quincy, when other responsibilities devolved on him. In 1858 he was elected by the Legislature warden of the State Penitentiary. His success in this trying position, was if anything more marked than in any of his preceding offices, and the State owes him a debt of gratitude for the valuable services rendered while managing the Penitentiary.

From the close of his term as warden until 1867, Mr. Pitman mingled little in politics or public affairs, but in the latter year his fellow citizens again elected him to the office of mayor of Quincy, in the hope that his rare judgment and foresight might extricate the city from the many embarrassments that were overwhelming it. Devoting himself for one year with the usual success to the work of relieving the city from the great burden of debt and taxation, he retired from the mayoralty, and at the same time from public life, preferring the ease and retirement of home to the bustle and din of political strife.

Possessed of large wealth, a man of genial and generous traits, enjoying the esteem and friendship of all who know him, his declining years are pregnant with unalloyed pleasure, and the worst wish that his fellow citizens harbor is, that he may long continue in the enjoyment of the happiness his industry, energy and ability have wrought for him.

BOILERS AND SHEET IRON WORKS.

We have said in a previous part of this work that in the manufacture of all kinds of machinery, Quincy took front rank among western cities, and as her boiler and sheet iron works are a part of this branch of manufactures, we claim the same superiority for them. Managed and superintended by experienced and skillful mechanics, all work from their establishments is turned out in a style unsurpassed any where. The most difficult work known to the trade, has been done successfully here within the past few years, and those who had been in the habit of sending east for extra heavy work, under the impression that it could not be turned out in the west, are now having the same done in the most workmanlike and satisfactory manner at home, and at a vast saving of price and freight.

The very best mechanics are employed in this line, and the most liberal enterprise is displayed by those engaged in the business. From the territory west of the Mississippi a constant demand is made upon them for work, and this demand increases so rapidly that even in the dull season now about closing, they have been taxed to their full capacity to keep pace with it. Moreover each winter another heavy demand is made upon these establishments by the steamers that lay up here at the close of navigation. There are a large number of these, and all require more or less repairing and new work, which they can have done here in a more satisfactory style and at more reasonable figures than at any point on the river. The St. Louis & Keokuk Packet Company, which owns and manages a large number of fine steamboats, long since discovered the advantages offered by Quincy in this respect, and annually harbors its steamers here through the winter to have them overhauled and repaired. The work done yearly by this company alone is an item of no small importance, and foots up handsomely.

Two establishments are now engaged in this branch of manufactures, and are owned and operated by the following firms:—John Williams & Co.; Oerter & Michelmann.

These firms employ together 85 hands, who turn out $18,000 worth of work per month, or $216,000 per year.

J. K. VanDOORN, MANUFACTURER & MERCHANT,

OR "MEN OF MARK IN QUINCY."

There is perhaps no city in the west whose leading citizens so early began to shape its moral course to an elevated standing, as Quincy. Her early settlers were men who came here to build up a model city, and with this object constantly before their minds, they aimed at the beginning to place the moral and social status of our city at the highest standard.

To this commendable work none have devoted more time or money than John K. VanDoorn, and there are none in the community, but award him credit for earnest efforts in this noble cause.

Coming from his native state, Massachusetts, in 1838, Mr. VanDoorn, then twenty-four years of age, commenced the manufacture of chairs with Mr. Mellen, they being the two partners in the humble establishment known as the "chair factory." Continuing at this for some time, he accumulated funds sufficient to purchase the saw mill on the river bank from E. B. Kimball. Soon after, he built a new mill on the site of the "Kimball Mill," and continued to operate it successfully, turning out a large quantity of lumber and building timber annually, until 1858, in which year it was destroyed by fire. Previous to its destruction, however, he had purchased an interest in the extensive saw mill on the bay, and became a partner in the same with James Arthur,

Esq. About this time also, he established himself in the lumber business, on Hampshire street, and made that also a success.

But while Mr. VanDoorn has been energetic and active as a manufacturer and merchant, and has achieved great pecuniary success, he has, as we have said, always had time and money to spare in behalf of every enterprise, promising to improve or elevate the moral and social status of Quincy.

An uncompromising advocate of temperance, he has been untiring in his opposition to license laws and the sale of intoxicating liquors. His convictions in this respect are the same to-day that first impressed his mind, and as the present Grand Worthy Secretary of the Good Templars of Illinois, he is doing herculean work in the cause. Also the first outspoken Abolitionist in Quincy, he continued earnestly and actively to advocate the emancipation of the slaves of the South, until that work was accomplished.

A man of strong convictions and determined character, he espouses whatever cause he engages in with a vigor and energy that at once indicates the rectitude of his purpose. Ever actuated by principle and yielding his convictions of right to no power or party, but boldly and persistently advocating them against all opposition, such a man is John K. VanDoorn, one of Quincy's most enterprising and valuable citizens. Through all his experiences as a business man and leading manufacturer, thorough integrity and honorable dealing have characterized him, and now, after a residence here of over 30 years, he ranks second to none in the esteem of his fellow citizens.

GAS—ITS INTRODUCTION INTO QUINCY.

OPERATIONS OF THE QUINCY GAS LIGHT & COKE COMPANY.

Those who are constantly consuming gas will perhaps be interested in a history of its introduction into our city and the operations of the Quincy Gas Light and Coke Company since its organization. The enterprise of lighting Quincy with gas and furnishing our citizens with this valuable illuminating article, like all new projects, was long discussed before any positive action was taken in regard to it. In 1853 a company was organized and a contract entered into by the corporators, John Wood, Lucius Kingman, Samuel Holmes, Thos. Redmond, Jas. D. Morgan, Samuel W. Rogers, Thos. C. King, Robert S. Benneson and William H. Carlin, with Messrs. A. B. Chambers and Thos. Pratt, of St. Louis, who, in consideration of $75,000 of the capital stock of the Quincy Gas Light and Coke Company, agreed to purchase suitable grounds, furnish all the materials and construct works of sufficient capacity to manufacture and store 55,000 cubic feet of gas daily, lay 3½ miles of street mains, provide the necessary meters, and erect 50 public lamps. At the same time a contract for fifty additional lamps, and in relation to extension and the right of way in laying street mains, was entered into. On the first of December, 1856, the contract for the erection of the works having been completed, and Messrs. Chambers & Pratt having purchased and erected 14 more lamps and furnished meters, seven pipes and other materials not specified in the contract, they were allowed an additional $5,100 in stock for extra labor and material. The whole stock of the company thus amounted to $80,100, and it commenced operating with one bench of three retorts, 64 public lamps and 139 private consumers. With the growth of the city the demand for gas has rapidly increased, and the company is now working eight benches of three retorts each to their full capacity, lighting 334 public lamps, supplying 750 private consumers, and has over eight and one-half miles of street mains. In 1867, a new gas holder 60 by 22 feet, with a capacity of 62,000 cubic feet was completed at a cost of $21,516.58. Since then the retort capacity of the company has been doubled, consisting of twelve benches of three retorts each, the old purifiers five feet six inches square, have been replaced by new ones ten by fourteen feet, and the old center seal of six inch capacity has been replaced with a new seal of ten inch capacity. The six inch street mains have been replaced by ten inch pipe, and the change has added materially to the pressure and flow of gas. The last mentioned improvements have cost the company $20,729.14, most of the work being done by Quincy mechanics.

The past year, the company with commendable enterprise, have run an eight inch pipe from the ten inch main on Hampshire street, along Seventh street to Broadway, and continued down the last named street with a six inch pipe to the levee. This work was done to accommodate patrons on Front street and the levee, who had suffered considerable inconvenience for want of a proper flow of gas, and while it cost the company $5,509, it added only one consumer.

The improvements at the works this year have been the introduction of new ten inch condensers with an exhauster and engine, at a combined cost of $6,610.76. The old gas holder was also repaired at a cost of $1,153, and is to be replaced the coming year by a new and improved one. Other improvements during the same period, including building, &c., aggregated $1,741.10.

The annual consumption of coal at the Gas Works is 77,763 bushels, and of lime 2,957 bushels. The pay roll proper amounts annually to $14,000. This company has now been in operation thirteen years, and although a majority of the stock is held in St. Louis, it has always been managed by Quincy men, who, while they have an interest in the pecuniary success of the company, have still a larger interest in operating it to the satisfaction of our citizens. Thus while they have acted in good faith as directors and managers, they have never failed to add such improvements as seemed in their judgment demanded by the city and their patrons.

In this particular therefore Quincy has a decided advantage. The capital stock now amounts to $101,550.

The enterprise exhibited by the company the past two years in laying new street mains and increasing its manufacturing capacity, is an earnest that they are determined to keep pace with the wants of the community, and supply our citizens with an article of gas not excelled any where. In this connection it is proper to state that there has been decided improvement.

The officers of the company at present, are :—J. D. Morgan, President; W. H. Corley, Superintendent and Secretary; H. R. Corley, Assistant Secretary; C. M. Pomroy, Treasurer; Directors, J. D. Morgan, W. H. Corley, C. M. Pomroy, Thomas Redmond, S. W. Rogers, R. S. Benneson, J. M. Pitman, L. Kingman, of Quincy, and Thomas Pratt of St. Louis.

H. V. SULLIVAN, ESQ.,

OR "MEN OF MARK" IN QUINCY.

It is a well established fact that the greatest lever for good or evil in any country is the press. The same is true doubtless of cities, for the press in municipal as well as national affairs possessess a power which if exerted for the right, is of vast benefit to a community. Nor is it venturing much to say that every city owes its progress in a large measure to its press. Newspapers are at once the evidence of civilization and enlightenment, and the means of heralding the virtues of every people, and the beauties of every locality to the world. But to wield their proper influence, and serve the community, newspapers require in their conduct able management and rare judgment. In this respect Quincy was superlatively fortunate in the acquisition of Henry V. Sullivan, Esq., one of its pioneer newspaper man.

Mr. Sullivan was born at Vincennes, Indiana, in 1816, and at the age of ten years moved to St. Louis. At sixteen he engaged as a printer in the office of the St. Louis *Republican*, and continued there for five years.— In 1836 he came to Quincy, and two years later commenced the publication of the Quincy *Whig*, although then only twenty-one years of age. At first the paper was owned by a stock company, but in a brief space of time Mr. Sullivan, associating with him S. M. Bartlett, bought up the stock, and run the establishment under the firm name of Bartlett & Sullivan. Nehemiah Bushnell and Andrew Johnson, volunteering their services as editors, managed that department for eight-months, when Mr. Bartlett assumed the duties of editor. On the death of Mr, Bartlett, in 1851, Mr. Sullivan managed and conducted the paper alone for one year, when he associated with him John T. Morton, and continued thus two years. On the 1st of January, 1857, he commenced the publication of the *Daily Republican*, under the firm name of H. V. Sullivan & Co., and continued for about 13 months.

While connected with the press, Mr. Sullivan was appointed Register of Lands, elected several times to the City Council of Quincy, and also to the Legislature of Illinois; in all of which positions he acquitted himself in such a manner as to win the admiration and retain the confidence of his fellow citizens.

At the outbreak of the war Mr. Sullivan received the appointment of paymaster, and gave his time and attion to the same while the strife lasted, when he returned to Quincy.

The publication of a newspaper in our city to-day may not be considered a herculean work, but in the days when the Quincy *Whig* began its existence, the struggle between life and death was a determined one; and had a less resolute or less judicious manager than Mr. Sullivan undertaken the work, the probability is that it would have flourished but briefly. As it was, the paper prospered, and gradually grew strong enough to be of vast use in building up the city that gave it birth, and nurtured it into strength. With Mr. Sullivan as its manager, it gave an earnest and vigorous support to every move in the interest of Quincy, and was instrumental in advancing the city morally, socially and commercially.

Although Mr. Sullivan has now virtually retired from business, he is still by no means on the decline of life, but on the contrary presents a hearty and healthy appearance, and is an active, enterprising and public spirited citizen, whose place could not well be filled in Quincy.

WAGONS, PLOWS, &c.

Early in our history, the manufacture of wagons, plows, and agricultural implements was commenced, and while it has steadily increased, it has also been marked by constant improvement. The reputation of our establishments in this line has long been first-class, and while their wagons, plows, &c. have been highly prized at home for their strength and durability, they have also been in demand in Missouri and regions west of the Mississippi. Near Quincy the best of timber for work in this line is to be had, and with the excellent mechanics who are drawn here by the inducements offered in wages and location, there could be no question of success for those engaged in the business.— Wherever anything of this kind is to be found, satisfaction follows, and hence the growing trade. Many of our most energetic and enterprising citizens are engaged in this department, and have in the course of their experience accumulated handsome fortunes, besides building up an extensive and permanent trade. Some of them began on a small scale it is true, but by close attention to business, and a liberal display of enterprise, have succeeded beyond their own anticipations. There is no difficulty in selling any article or implement turned out by them, and they have consequently flourished with remarkable success. At present the following firms are engaged in this line, and while several of these are modest concerns, there are also a number of extensive manufacturers, who employ each a large number of hands :—W. T. & E. A. Rogers; T. Beatty; Bolinger & Grussenmeyer; Brinkkoeter & Benhof; W. Herlemann; G. Keller; H. Knapheide; F. Meise; H. Nolkemper; L. Otten; T. Otto; A. C. Root; Schefer & Ledig; L. Schmitt; F. Tafelski.

These firms are all doing a handsome business, and employing skillful mechanics are almost daily introducing some new improvement, that gives them a further hold upon their numerous patrons. This year these firms have turned out over 700 wagons, besides plows, &c. The capital invested amounts to $260,000.

PLANING MILLS.

Quincy now boasts establishments prepared to turn out almost any article or implement used in mechanism or commerce, and she is, if possible, better prepared with materials for building purposes. Although our city is built up almost exclusively of brick, yet we keep a large number of planing mills busy supplying doors, sash, and flooring. They also manufacture largely for the Missouri and western trade, and are constantly shipping large quantities off by river and rail. We have now in operation three large and capacious planing mills, which are ably managed by skillful and experienced business men, and are doing handsomely.— Besides those which are immediately in the city, we have still another, owned and operated by citizens of Quincy, but located on the west bank of the river. This has been recently established by Bradford, McCoy & Co.

These establishments all turn out first-class work, and are run in model style. They are owned and operated by the following firms:—Bradford, McCoy & Co.; Gould & Williams; Schmitt, Mulliner & Co.; Menke, Grimm & Co.

These firms employ an aggregate force of 116 men, and manufacture annually $310,600 worth of doors, sash, flooring &c. Capital invested, $180,000.

BRICK.

The manufacture of brick is necessarily carried on very extensively in Quincy, as the great majority of our buildings are built of that material. There is perhaps no city in the Union where there is such a preponderance of brick over frame buildings—hence the great security here from fire. At all our yards they turn out excellent brick, as they obtain splendid clay for that purpose in all quarters, and have the very best chance for making them equal to the finest brick found anywhere. During the summer these yards employ a large number of hands, and thus are of a double benefit to the city. Brick are sold here at reasonable rates, and buildings of this kind are built at a small increase over frame buildings.

This season the following firms have been engaged in making brick:—J. H. Konefes; Brinkhoff & Forke; A. J. Casebeer; G. Damhorst; S. Damhorst; F. W. Freese; F. Hagerman; Honor & Holtmann; J. A. Hummert; J. H. Koch; H. Landwehr; J. Menne; C. L. Prante; J. H. Sander.

They employ upwards of 300 hands, and sell annually $616,000 worth of brick.

GEN. JAMES D. MORGAN,

OR "MEN OF MARK" IN QUINCY.

During the late war the patriotism of Quincy shone out with a luster that even the protracted and desperate nature of the conflict failed to dim. Many of her sons, young and old, sprang to the front at the first alarm, and remained there steadfast in defense of the Union, or fell in the cause. Of these none achieved greater eminence, or rendered more valuable service, than Gen. James D. Morgan, whose record as a soldier is a bright page in the history of the war.

Born in Boston in 1810, in 1834 he cast his fortunes with Quincy, and worked at his trade as a cooper, Edward Wells, Esq., being employed in the same shop. The following spring, in connection with the last named gentlemen, he rented a shop that stood where the jail now stands, and they thus commenced the cooperage business for themselves. We next find him engaged in the confectionery business under the Quincy House. About this time his military experiences began, and being captain of a militia company, he was ordered to Hancock county, the scene of the Mormon excitement. In 1846 he volunteered for the war with Mexico, and went immediately to the front, as captain of "A" Company, 1st Reg. Ill. Vol., commanded by the gallant Hardin. Returning to Quincy at the close of the war, in 1847, at the breaking out of the late war, he promptly enlisted in a company then being raised here, and, with a modesty proverbial of the man, accepted the position of orderly sergeant, though tendered and urged to accept a more exalted rank. Proceeding to Cairo with his company, he was at once called by the unanimous voice of the famous 10th Reg. Ill. Inf, to the position of lieutenant colonel. On the promotion of Gen. B. M. Prentiss, its colonel, to the command of a brigade, Gen. Morgan was at once advanced to the colonelcy. His regiment soon after took the field, and began its glorious career of five years service, during which time the valor and endurance of its men were tried on many an ensanguined field and weary march. Bird's Point, New Madrid, Corinth, Mission Ridge, Chicamauga, Berton's Hill, &c., are inscribed upon its banners, and attest the determined courage and confidence of these heroes, when led by their "old commander." At the last named place Gen. Morgan was brevetted major general for gallant conduct. He also participated with his regiment in Sherman's famous march to the sea, and retired from the army with a record that will bear comparison with any of the veterans, whose achievements have inscribed their names upon the roll of honor, and won the admiration of the nation. For over four years Gen. Morgan was with his regiment all the time, asking for no leave of absence and accepting none, but ever present with his men, devoted to their welfare, and zealous in their behalf. No commander was ever more beloved and idolized, and none ever reciprocated that affection more generously than he.

These were the achievements of war; but successful as has been Gen. Morgan in military affairs, his civil career has been not less marked and interesting. A partner for twenty-five years in the firm of C. M. Pomroy & Co., doing an extensive business in packing pork, he also took an active interest in the progress of the city, and has given generously of his time and wealth to advance many of our public enterprises. One of the first to enlist our citizens in the project of introducing gas into the city, also a moving spirit in building the great "Rink," and the stately Opera House, he has been no less active in behalf of others of a more extensive character, such as railroads, steamboat lines, &c.

A man of genial temperament, quiet, but energetic and confident, Gen. Morgan has no superior as a business man, while as a part of the social and moral element of Quincy, he is invaluable.

ST. MARY'S HOSPITAL.

Hospitals are perhaps the last institutions in the world that people in the course of their wanderings would dream of visiting. There seems a natural aversion upon the part of humaity to gaze upon others in distress or sickness, or witness the operation of ills, to which they are heirs. Of the native instinct that bids us to keep aloof from the sick and distressed, we are not to speak, but, on the contrary, our object is to speak of an institution, in the success of which all our citizens have an abiding interest, and which is a noble monument to the cause of charity.

A little over two years ago a small delegation of Sisters of Charity visited Quincy from a neighboring city for the purpose of determining the feasibility of erecting here a hospital where the sick and distressed of every clime and creed would find a home in their troubles, and be cared for and nursed by kind Sisters, who, self-sacrificingly, had devoted their lives to this charitable work. A brief visit satisfying them that our people, ever generous and open-hearted, were charitably disposed, they at once decided upon erecting here a hospital equal to the wants of our flourshing city. Ground was at once obtained at a reasonable price on Broadway, between Thirteenth and Fourteenth streets, on the south side, and after the good Sisters of St. Francis had, from donations and collections received here and elsewhere, accummulated a sum sufficient to encourage them in the success of their enterprise, they at once began the erection of the building.

Plans were advertised for, and one best suited to the tastes and ideas of the proper committee, was fixed upon as the model for the building. The present structure is the result of the designs. Its exterior appearance surpasses almost every other building in the city, and we doubt whether the State furnishes an edifice constructed for a like sum that presents half as imposing an appearance. Three stories high with cut stone basement under the entire building, and a Mansard roof surmounting the whole, it towers up grand and lofty on Broadway, one of the most desirable streets in the city. Before describing the interior we will state that it was built at a cost of $35,000, which considering the style and dimensions of the structure, was very cheap.

The interior of this, like all institutions of its kind, is the most interesting feature as we are thus enabled to observe the practical operations to which it is devoted.

The first floor of the hospital is divided up into seven spacious apartments: the first of which that attracts the attention of the visitor, is the neat and pleasant reception room immediately to the right of the entrance; a few steps further on, and we find a pair of comfortably but not gorgeously furnished parlors—a drug store and reading room, also occupy a portion of this floor, and are each model departments. Besides these are rooms for the sisters, and a few apartments for the sick.

The second floor is almost exclusively used for patients.

On the third floor the arrangements are somewhat different from the second, owing to the fact that it is devoted to the use of female invalids. In addition to the ordinary apartments there is on this floor a large and well ventilated room, which is used as a sewing department.

The fourth floor, which is under the Mansard roof, is a fine airy story, and is divided into wash rooms, baggage rooms, &c. Every floor has a neat and well arranged bath room, with all the modern appliances and improvements and water closets.

The basement contains the kitchen and dining rooms and is also high and airy. A furnace for heating the entire house with hot air is also located here. In every story and every department the hospital is complete, and with its neat and cosy furniture, its sanded floors and polished paint tells of the industry and taste of the sisters in charge.

Although the institution is under the immediate control of the Catholics, and has a chapel for the use of those who profess that faith, still, of the occupants of the institution there are Episcopalians, Methodists, &c., and those professing no faith. They are all furnished with good moral reading, but no undue influence is brought to bear upon patients to convert them to the faith of the sisters in charge.

SADDLES AND HARNESS.

There is scarcely a street in Quincy that does not boast an immense saddle and harness establishment; and large numbers of men are employed here in this line of manufacturing. The goods turned out are of the best material, and manufactured in a style that for workmanship and durability is not to be excelled. A large section of the west is supplied from these establishments, and orders come here constantly from the most extreme Southern States. During the war an extensive business in the manufacture of army equipments was carried on here, and our colossal factories and shops were alive with employees—several firms having as high as two hundred hands at work. With the close of the war business again sought its legitimate channels, and a consequent reduction in employees followed at all these establishments. Since then a fair trade has been carried on, and the prospect is encouraging for a rapid increase from this time forward.

At present the following firms are engaged in the manufacture of saddles, harness &c.:—S. L. Taylor; Boon & Tillson; Campbell Bros.; H. Head, Sr.; B. Koch & Son; H. Messerschmidt; X. Neumann; Scheiner & Kreitz; Smith & Starling; Henry Steinkamp; Taylor & Co.; A. B. Wilhelm; Jacob Metz; T. H. Musser.

These firms employ 180 hands, and do an annual business in manufacturing of $233,400.

ENOCH COMSTOCK, LEADING MANUFACTURER,

OR "MEN OF MARK" IN QUINCY.

Eminent as has been the success of our citizens in commerce, finances and statesmanship, it was reserved for her to reach the acme of her fame through the achievements of her manufacturers. While her extensive factories, dusky foundries, and stately mills have added largely to our wealth as a city, they have also been the scenes of the struggles and triumphs of many of our most valuable citizens.

Prominent among those who have devoted themselves successfully to building up our manufacturing interests, stands the subject of this sketch, Enoch Comstock, Esq.

A native of Massachusetts, in 1837 Mr. Comstock came west, and located in Quincy, opening a small tinshop on the site of the handsome block recently erected by I. V. W. Dutcher, Esq. Three hundred dollars comprised the capital with which he commenced business. The spring following, Allen Comstock, a brother, arrived from the east, and together, under the name of Comstock & Co., they commenced the stove and tinware business. Continuing in this business until 1850, Mr.

Allen Comstock embarked in the enterprise of manufacturing stoves, opening a foundry, with Frederick Collins, Esq., as a partner. This arrangement was however of short duration—the foundry and store soon consolidating, under the proprietorship and management of the original firm of Comstock & Co. The business was operated thus until 1860, when the loss of over $30,000 by the revulsions of 1857-8, made it necessary to increase the capital in order to operate profitably and successfully. Messrs. F. Collins, T. H. Castle, and C. H. Winn were then induced to take an interest, and the business was again continued under the firm name of Collins, Comstock & Co, and under the same able management. This firm was dissolved by limitation on the 1st day of February, 1869. Re-organizing the firm at this date, with Enoch Comstock as senior member, it continued the extensive and increasing business with the same skill and sagacity that characterized its predecessors; and to-day, it is if possible more prosperous and active than ever. With a foundry equal in size to any in the west, and not surpassed any where for accommodations and conveniences; with a force of nearly two hundred hands constantly at work, and with a vast territory to supply with the products of their establishments, we venture little in stating that few firms anywhere have as brilliant prospects before them as Comstock, Castle & Co.

During the last nine years, their trade has grown to magnificent proportions, and the demands upon them have been so heavy and constant, that they have been compelled to make repeated additions to their foundry, and enlarge its capacity, until the present time, when we find the company prepared to melt with ease 1,800 tons per year.

Nor has this been all; while this company has brought success and wealth to those who organized it, it has also accomplished much for Quincy. Bringing here hundreds of citizens, and affording them employment at liberal wages, it has also been the means of introducing us abroad, and thus attracting many to Quincy as a base of supplies. Here too has been built up one of the great stove markets of the country, for which we are indebted to the energy and enterprise of the Messrs. Comstock, who have struggled for years to accomplish that desired consummation.

Although long years in the traces, and ever active and industrious as a business man, still Mr. Comstock is to-day a comparatively young man, full of life and energy, and destined to long service in the extensive business he has been so prominent in building up.— Genial and sociable, enterprising and public spirited, Quincy has no more estimable and valuable citizen than Enoch Comstock.

ICE.

The ice interest of Quincy has within a few years loomed up into magnificent proportions, absorbing a large amount of capital, and giving employment to a large number of men every season. Upwards of twenty firms are now packing or dealing in ice at this point, and a commendable degree of activity is displayed in the business. The quality of the ice packed here is equal to any furnished in the country. It is cut principally in Quincy Bay, which shoots off from the Mississippi, and extends north about one mile, where the "Crystal Springs" pour their limpid and translucent waters into it. In the vicinity of these springs are built the principal ice houses of the city, and here the most extensive packing is done. The ice cut in this vicinity is usually from sixteen to twenty inches in thickness. No clearer, purer, or more solid ice than is taken out here is to be found, and being packed in an admirable manner, it meets with a prompt sale at good figures. The amount annually packed is upwards of 50,000 tons; and this business, which a few years since was monopolized by a single house, employing a dozen hands, and two or three teams, has grown to colossal proportions, absorbing a vast amount of capital, and employing hundreds of hands and teams. Much of the ice put up here is shipped south during the summer, and our southern patrons find it superior to any that reaches them. The men engaged in this enterprise are all active and energetic, and are destined to still greater success than they have yet achieved.

HENRY ROOT, ESQ., PRESIDENT UNION BANK.

OR "MEN OF MARK" IN QUINCY.

It is perhaps fortunate for Quincy, that none, or at least but few, of her prominent citizens acquired their wealth, or any portion of the same, by inheritance.— With scarce an exception, all those who have made their mark in law, commerce, or finance here, commenced the struggle of life with energy, industry, and a fair share of ability only, to guarantee them success in the strife for fortune and happiness.

Of this class was Henry Root, Esq., now President of the Union Bank of Quincy, one of our wealthiest and most influential citizens. A native of Canada, at the early age of twenty he decided to make the United States his home, and came to Chicago in 1836. From there he went to St. Louis, and to Palmyra, Mo., and in 1840 arrived in Quincy, with a capital amounting to a little less than one dollar. Having however good credit, he at once embarked in the mercantile business, selling goods also at auction. Continuing in this line for a short period, he associated with him James Fisher, and went into the regular mercantile business, under the firm name of Root & Fisher. Disposing of his interest in the firm in 1847, Mr. Root accepted the sutlership of a regiment raised for the United States army in Mexico, commanded by Col. E. W. B. Newby, and proceeded with it to Santa Fe. Returning to Quincy in 1848, in 1849 he went to New Orleans, and made a heavy purchase of sugar and molasses, which was shipped up the river, and arrived at St. Louis just in time to be destroyed by the great fire of that year.— Effecting a compromise with the insurance companies, by which he secured one-half the insurance money, he again returned to Quincy, and resumed the mercantile business, with N. T. Lane as a partner. At the expiration of two years he purchased the interest of Mr. Lane in the establishment, and conducted it alone through an uninterrupted career of prosperity until 1865, when he disposed of the same and retired from mercantile life.

In 1867, Mr. Root purchased one-sixth interest in the Illinois State Penitentiary, and subsequently acquired four-sixths of that institution, but the same year surrendered his entire interest to the State.

Realizing in common with many leading citizens the necessity for greater banking facilities in Quincy, in 1869 Mr. Root, in connection with other capitalists of our city, established the Union Bank of Quincy, of which he was elected President, and which commenced operations under the most favorable auspices the present year. A man of ripe sagacity and rare judgment, thoroughly versed in the finances and commerce of the country, Quincy affords no citizen better calculated to manage the affairs of a bank with mutual satisfaction and profit to patrons and stockholders.

As a citizen, Mr. Root has been second to none in public spirit and enterprise, and after a business career of nearly thirty years, he enjoys the friendship and esteem of the entire community. Pleasant and inviting in conversation, generous and genial in oppearance and disposition, his social qualities are as marked as his business sagacity.

THE RINK.

FINEST BUILDING OF THE KIND IN AMERICA.

Some eighteen months ago Mr. J. B. Thompson, of the firm of Hervey, Johnson & Co., patentees and sole builders of Hervey's Patent Skating Rink, arrived in Quincy, with a view to enlisting our citizens in the enterprise of erecting in this city a skating rink, to exceed in size and magnificence any similar establishment in America. He knew the reputation of our citizens for pride, ambition and energy, and knew how to present the matter in a form that would most probably secure favorable consideration from those who could provide means to make the enterprise a success. At first he had some difficulty in securing the earnest attention of our capitalists, but at length they were satisfied that the rink was an institution needed by the public, and that it would pay. When this conclusion was arrived at, it took no time at all to secure subscriptions of stock to the amount of $15,000. The stock holders at once formed a permanent organization by the election of Gen. J. D. Morgan, President, C. H. Bull, Vice President, and Thomas T. Woodruff Secretary and Treasurer. These gentlemen, together with Messrs William McFadden, C. E. Whitmore, E. J. Parker, J. B. Thompson, Col. Chas. H. Morton, and Gen. Wm. A. Schmitt, constitute the present Board of Directors. In the election, which was held one hundred and sixty shares were represented in the vote. The Board having appointed the President and Messrs Bull and McFadden a building committee, they, the committee, proceeded at once to secure a site for the building, and succeeded in leasing on good terms the property on Ninth and Jersey streets, and contracted with Messrs. Hervey, Johnson & Co., for the erection of a suitable building. The work was commenced at once, and progressed rapidly and steadily under the immediate supervision of Mr. J. H. A. Hervey, by whom, also, the very handsome rinks at St. Louis, Chicago and Cincinnati were erected. The building is located 105 feet from the corner of Jersey street, and is two hundred and forty feet in length by eighty-five in width, and forty-eight in height. The floor or ice surface is 178 by 71 feet, giving about 13,000 square feet of ice. The ice bed a perfectly smooth and level surface of blue clay. The wells on the ground together with the springs on the high ground in the vicinity of the rink furnish an ample supply of water at all times. The water is conveyed from the springs in pipes. By this arrangement they are able to flood the whole building with water at a few moments notice. When the ice is once formed it lasts a long time, a single inch of ice on a blue clay bed furnishing good skating to hundreds of persons for sometimes six weeks at a stretch.

The arrangements for light, ventilation, &c., in the building are very complete. On each side there are two tiers of windows, the lower tier having thirteen windows, with twelve lights in each. The upper one in the cupola has the same number of windows, with twenty-four lights in each. In the front are twelve windows with twelve lights each, and four circular windows, making in all twelve hundred panes of glass in the building. When illuminated on a winter night with one hundred and forty jets of gas, the building presents a gay and most animating spectacle. In the center of the east end of the edifice there is a gallery of appropriate dimensions for the use of the musicians. Around the entire room is a promenade seven feet in width. Two rows of seats are arranged along this fine walk, capable of accommodating at least six hundred people. The ice bed is about three feet below this, access thereto being afforded by means of a stairway at each corner. The main apartment is indeed a grand room, lofty and spacious, and with something of the sublime in the vast and beautiful arched roof, quite unobstructed by unsightly beams and timbers, the vast space being spanned only by a few iron rods, which are not really necessary, but are put there to gratify the imagination of the people, and allay any fears as to the strength and safety of the roof.

The principal entrance to the rink is on Ninth street, by a large double door. The entrance hall is twelve by eight feet, upon one side of the Director's room and ticket office with two windows. Next to that is the ladies' parlor, which is twenty-two by twelve feet in size, and is elegantly furnished. Adjoining this is a dressing and wash room, supplied with all things necessary for arranging the toilet. The gentleman's parlor is the same size as the other.

The outside of the building is covered with two coats of drab paint, and is ornamented by a rich cornice.

The roof is a perfect arch, the spans supporting it being two semi-circles, eighty-four feet in diameter.

In the lower part of the sides of the building are the windows or doors for ventilation or freezing the air, passing through them under the promenade, and into the main hall under the ice, thereby making the temperature the same in all parts of the room,

The grounds were leased to the association for five years, at a rental of six per cent. of the value of the ground which is $35 per foot, with the privilege of purchasing at these figures any time within five years.

Thus by the spirit and enterprise of a number of our leading citizens, Quincy secured a place of resort for the young and old of our city, where the exhilarating pastime of skating is indulged with every security of life, and also with a management that provides such restrictions and regulations as will guard the moral and social atmosphere surrounding the same. We know of no institution better calculated to enhance the pleasures of life in Quincy than this, and therefore mention it with pride.

CHARLES A. SAVAGE. PRES'T Q. M. & P. R. R.,

OR "MEN OF MARK" IN QUINCY.

Quincy is vastly indebted to her railway system for much that she is and expects to be. True, she had the grand old Mississippi flowing before her to the sea; but this great artery of commerce, while it is invaluable as an auxiliary to prosperity, was not sufficient to advance our city with the rapidity that has attended its growth. Our railroads have without doubt been the most potent in forwarding our city in commerce and manufactures, and we naturally turn to the men who have been prominent in conceiving and constructing them.

Foremost among them stands Charles A Savage, President of the Quincy, Missouri & Pacific Railroad.

A native of Maine, Mr. Savage after graduating at Bowdoin College, in 1837, and being admitted to the bar at Bangor, in 1839, came to Quincy in the latter year, being then 24 years of age. Admitted to the bar here, he promptly set to work, and soon after received the appointment of Illinois agent of the Munn Illinois Land Company, in which capacity, and in a general land agency, he continued to a recent date.

In the year 1848, the old State Bank of Illinois having closed up its business, and there being no institution furnishing banking facilities on the Mississippi River north of St. Louis, Mr. Savage, in company with Newton Flagg and I. O. Woodruff, established a banking house, and continued in that business for many years. A man of powerful mind, and great foresight, he early saw the importance of making Quincy the center of the railroad system that was seeking connection with the Mississippi. One of the original movers in the project of building the Quincy & Toledo, Quincy & Palmyra, and the Quincy & Chicago railroads, he was for a number of years President of the first, Director of the second up to its consolidation with the Hannibal & St. Joe, and for a long period treasurer of the third.

With others Mr. Savage organized the Meredosia Bridge Company, to bridge the Illinois River for railroad purposes, and was president of that company.— With other prominent citizens of Quincy he also took the initiatory steps in the organization of the Quincy Railroad Bridge Companies of Missouri and Illinois, and was one of the first Directors. After their consolidation he was chosen Secretary of the Company, and continued as such until the final completion of the grand structure which now spans the Mississippi River at this point.

Such is a brief record of the activity displayed by Charles A. Savage, in enterprises that have now become successful, and are monuments of his sagacity and foresight; but in others now being projected, with the most encouraging prospects of early completion, he has been if anything more active and zealous than in the former.

Within the past two years he has filled the position of Secretary of the Quincy & Warsaw Railroad; has been President of the Quincy, Alton & St. Louis Railway Company, has acted as Director of the Toledo, Wabash & Western, and is now as we have said, President of the Quincy, Missouri & Pacific Railway.

Moreover, Mr. Savage, although devoting much of his time to enterprises such as the above, has been second to none in his zeal for the moral and social advancement of Quincy. A christian gentleman of the noblest type, he has munificently aided the charitable, educational and religious institutions of our city, and has at all times been the friend of science and art.

Of pleasant and affable address, of rare judgment and thorough business qualifications, a deep thinker and sagacious observer, he wields a large influence with the leading men of Quincy, and is admired and esteemed by all who know him.

AGRICULTURAL IMPLEMENTS.

Where such an extent of rare farming land is to be found, the manufacture of agricultural implements and machines, ought certainly to meet with success, and be carried forward on a large scale. We regret to admit that in this respect Quincy has not developed her energies as rapidly as in other departments of manufactures. True, those engaged in this branch are among the most enterprising and active of our manufacturers, but there are not enough of them to give our city eminence as a manufacturing mart for agricultural machines and implements. Whatever is undertaken here is energetically carried on, and those who have embarked in this branch of manufactures have been successful beyond their most sanguine anticipations.

We have now three firms engaged in turning out work in this line, and they find little difficulty in competing with other localities. They employ annually a large number of hands, pay liberal wages, and turn out work that for finish, durability and use are not excelled anywhere.

These firms are Joshua S. Wood & Co.; W. T. & E. A. Rogers; and Battell & Collins.

The two latter firms do an extensive business in the manufacture and sale of all kinds of plows, and are busy the year round filling orders.

The firm of Joshua S. Wood & Co. is engaged in a specialty; manufacturing only the celebrated Vandiver Corn Planter. In this they have been vastly successful. Commencing work in 1865, their sales in that year amounted to only 550. In 1866 they increased to 800, in 1867 to 1,100, and the present year it will require over 2000 to fill their orders.

This firm employs a capital of $50,000, and works 80 hands.

HON. C. A. WARREN,

OR "MEN OF MARK" IN QUINCY.

The bar of Adams County, it is well known, has been prolific of great legal minds: but of all the gifted and erudite lawyers who have been prominent in our courts, none have been more eminent for ability and versatility than the subject of this sketch.

Hon. Calvin A. Warren was born in New York, in 1807, and first saw the light of day in a Court House, his father being sheriff of the county; which, considering the events since transpiring, and the ardor with which he has devoted himself to the law, to say the least, forms a singular coincidence. Receiving a common school education, at an early age he entered a printing office in the capacity of "devil," and continued in that position until he perfected himself in the art, and was rewarded with a *case*. Soon after he obtained employment in the *Spectator* office, at Salem, New York, and there for several months worked side by side with Horace Greely, of the New York *Tribune*, who has since won such fame as an editor and politician. While following the vocation of printer, Mr. Warren devoted himself also assiduously to the study of law, and in 1828-9, retiring from the case, he proceeded to Hampshire, N. Y., and assumed the editorial management of the Hampshire *Sentinel and Farmers' Journal*. Here he remained until 1830, when in connection with his brother, A. Warren, he published the *Palladium*, at West Troy, N. Y. An uncompromising democrat, he soon after removed to Ballston Spa, Saratoga County, and established another paper in the interest of that party; but the entire establishment being destroyed by fire, in the following spring, he associated with one of the proprietors of the *Spectator*, and established a paper at Belchester, N. Y. In 1833, after a varied career in the newspaper business, he entered Transylvania Law University, at Lexington, Kentucky, where he graduated with high honors in the latter part of 1834. He received his first diploma the same year from the Supreme Court of Ohio, and commenced the practice of law at Batavia, in that State, with Thomas Morris, (father of Hon. I. N. Morris, of this city, and afterwards United States Senator from Ohio,) as a partner. Resolving to seek a home further west, in 1836 Mr. Warren came to this city, and after practicing law one year, removed to Warsaw, where he remained until 1839, when he returned to Quincy, and formed a law partnership with James H. Ralston, which continued some two years.— Almeron Wheat, Esq., then associated with the firm, which now flourished under the style of Ralston, Warren & Wheat. Upon the dissolution of this firm, Mr. Warren associated with Hon. O. C. Skinner, continuing with him until that gentleman was elected Supreme Judge, when he formed a partnership with George Edmonds, Jr., of Hancock County. This partnership lasted for several years, when Mr. Edmonds moving to

Hancock County, Mr. Warren associated with Hon. Alexander E. Wheat, his present partner. An almost unprecedented career of success has attended this firm, and they have been engaged in most of the celebrated cases that have transpired in our courts for a number of years.

Returning to the time Col. Warren lived in Warsaw, we find that he owned one-third of all the land on which that city now stands; also owned and controlled the first hotel and livery stable, and started the first brick yard there. He also conducted a large store, supplying not only the citizens of Warsaw and the surrounding country, but also the Indians for many miles around, with goods, amunition, &c. About this time he also chartered a steamer at Cincinnati, and loading it with an assorted cargo, made a successful trip around to Warsaw. Buying a large farm, he also managed that, but several bad seasons blasted his hopes in this line.

In 1855 he returned to Quincy and embarked in manufacturing, building an extensive furniture factory near the site where the Union Passenger Depot now stands. Scarcely was this completed when it was destroyed by fire, envolving a loss upon the owner of $30,000. Not discouraged, however, he at once proceeded to replace the building consumed, and immediately erected the large building now occupied by Harris, Beebe & Co., on Fifth and Ohio streets. Here he resumed the manufacture of furniture, but the crash of 1857 coming on, the enterprise proved unsuccessful.

Thus have we noted many of the events in the career of Calvin A. Warren, as an editor, merchant, farmer, and manufacturer. His achievements as a lawyer have however been more marked, and this profession has been the crowning success of his life.

A man of versatile talent, quick wit and shrewd judgment, he seems molded for success in every department of law—while the same rare gifts have made him also a prominent feature of the social element of Quincy.

THE QUINCY RAILROAD BRIDGE.

A STUPENDOUS ENTERPRISE—A GREAT ENGINEERING TRIUMPH.

In view of the great and extending interests of the western trade, the importance of an uninterrupted railway crossing of the Mississippi, which would overcome the difficulties of low water in summer, and of the ice blockade of winter, was long appreciated by the enterprising city of Quincy. Her sagacious business men foresaw the gigantic inter-oceanic trade that seeking an east and west transit on an unbroken line, would tolerate no intermediate department, and would subject to its iron sway the mountain, the desert, and the river. Rising superior to mere local views, and in the interests of universal commerce, as well as to make secure their admirable location on the future highway, they invited public attention to the superior facilities for bridging the Mississippi at Quincy. As early as 1855, a charter for this purpose, drafted by Col. Samuel Holmes, one of the earliest friends of the measure. and pressed by a large number of public spirited citizens, was obtained from the State Legislature. The crisis of 1857, and the absorbing and protracted civil war which subsequently intervened, prevented however the prosecution of the project, and the charter was suffered to expire by limitation. Its old friends and advocates, prominent among whom may be named without invidiousness Ex-Gov. Wood, C. A. Savage, N. Bushnell, J. M. Pitman, Col. S. Holmes, and Thos. Redmond, still fondly cherished their enterprising conception, and at the session of 1864-5, Mr. Redmond, at that time a representative from Adams County, succeeded in procuring a re-enactment of the act of incorporation from the Legislature of Illinois. The sanction of the National Government being deemed of the utmost importance, the task of securing it was devolved on Ex-Gov. John Wood, the founder and patriarch of the city, to whose liberality and public spirit it owes a large measure of its prosperity, and to whose national as well as local reputation in connection with the history of Illinois and the war for the Union, his exalted patriotism, sterling integrity of character, and tireless energy in the prosecution of the important trust committed to him, Quincy is indebted for this grand and crowning contribution to her advancement, his great influence, and faithful and persevering efforts having been chiefly instrumental in obtaining the passage of the requisite act of Congress in face of the most formidable and persistent opposition from rival interests. The incorporators under the act were John Wood, Samuel Holmes, James M. Pitman, and N. Bushnell, and the charter thus obtained, of the amplest character, granting equal privileges to all railroads, present or future, to avail themselves of any bridge constructed under its provisions on just and impartial terms, and also carefully guarding the important interests of navigation.

The important pre-requisite of obtaining both State and National sanction having been triumphantly achieved, the next step was to secure the realization of the project. To this end was invited the co-operation of the three railroads having termini in Quincy—the Chicago, Burlington & Quincy, the Toledo, Wabash & Western, and the Hannibal & St. Joseph, and after several conferences, an arrangement was happily perfected in November, 1866, between the incorporators and the managers of the roads named, under which a union of their joint energies and efforts was effected for the prosecution of the great enterprise. Under this arrangement the Bridge Company was at once organized with N. Bushnell, of Quincy, James F. Joy, President of the C. B. & Q. R. R., Warren Colburn, Vice President T. W. & W. R. W., E. A. Chapin, Gen. Sup't T. W. & W. R, W., and John Lathrop, Treasurer H. & St. Jo. R. R., as Directors, who at a subsequent meeting perfected the organization by the appointment of the following officers: Nehemiah Bushnell, President; Warren Colburn, Vice President; Charles A. Savage, Secretary; Amos T. Hall, Treasurer, and Newton Flagg, Assistant Treasurer and General Agent.

It was determined by the Company that the bridge they were organized to construct should be a model structure, perfect, solid, permanent, and in every way worthy of its important position on the great thoroughfare of the world's commerce. To this end the first engineering talent of America was invoked, and after due and careful deliberation, the conception and execution of the mighty work was entrusted to the following able and experienced board of engineers: 'Warren Colburn, consulting engineer; Thomas C. Clarke, chief engineer; Col. E. D. Mason, first assistant engineer and superintendent of construction; and George Wolcott and H. H. Killaly, assistant engineers.

In devising the plan for the proposed bridge, several important considerations were involved requiring more than usual deliberation, and the employment of the best engineering skill. The river to be spanned was broad and capricious, noted for the general swiftness of its current, which rose to impetuosity during high water, and when concentered within its channel bounds during the low stages, for its immense masses of floating ice and the frequent terriffic disruption of vast ice-gorges at the breaking up in the spring, for its shifting sands and for its increasing tendency to abrade and wear away its banks. Of paramount importance moreover, was the necessity of paying due regard to the interests of navigation, and in view of the disasters of which other bridges on the river had been the prolific cause, to use every possible precaution against similar accicidents, and by providing ample, easy, and secure passage way for the customary water craft, obviate the well-founded apprehensions which had hitherto existed in the minds of river men in regard to bridging the Mississippi. To accommodate opposing interests, as well as to overcome natural obstacles and impediments, in a spirit of liberality and enterprise which reflects favorably on American railway management, and is well worthy of the great corporations chiefly interested, and of the magnitude of the duty they had undertaken, the Bridge Company gave their engineer corps a *carte blanche* as to cost, limited only by the accomplishment fully, perfectly, and completely, of all the objects to be attained. With what ability, faithfulness and success these instructions were fulfilled, and with what wise economy in view of the great ends accomplished the work was consummated, the grand structure is itself a noble witness, and may be claimed with just pride by its constructors, as the most perfect and successful enterprise of its class in the United States.

The extreme care in regard to the river interests is evidenced by the location of the bridge with special reference to the steamboat channel, all diagonalism having been avoided and the most perfect and complete parallel to the flow of the current having been established by persistent triangulation. The success in this respect has been marked as well as satisfactory, as proved by the facility with which the largest class of steamboats have made the passage since its completion over one year ago, and, together with the faithful compliance with the act of congress in respect to the height of bridge above the highest known water, the spacious and perfectly manageble draw-bridge, the ample space between the more important piers on the channel side of the river, and the extra span of 200 feet on the east shore especially allowed for rafting purposes during high water in compliance with request, although involving a change of plan after the work was in progress, proved the liberal and accommodating spirit of the company and elicited unanimous and unqualified commendation from every class of the river trade.

In determining upon the important point of the site of the bridge a thorough scientiffic exploration was made of both banks of the river for the distance of two miles from the extreme northern to the southern limits of the city, which finally resulted in the present admirable location, the superiority of which, everything considered, has been fully demonstrated in the completion and success of the enterprise. The point at which the great crossing leaves the Quincy side is at the foot of Spruce street, in the northwest part of the city, where the intervention of the bay and island divided the distance to be overcome into comparatively easy sections, where the west bank presented the most elevated and eligible point, and where soundings established a solid rock bottom in the channel of the river for the all-important main or pivot pier. The great or main bridge, spanning the river from the island to the west bank, is 3185 feet in length. Its superstructure is of iron of the Pratt Truss, which years of trial has proved to be the best form for strength, durability and lightness. It rests upon nineteen piers of best quality of first class cut stone masonry. The foundation of all the water piers, except the centre or pivot pier, is of piles driven to refusal and cut off eight feet below low water. The foundation of the pivot pier is the solid rock in the bed of the river. The foundation of piles is supported by a filling of concrete to their top, on which is first placed a solid platform of a triple thickness of twelve-inch timbers, laid diagonally and firmly bolted together, on which five feet below the lowest known water, commences the cut stone masonry, the bottom course of 2-foot stone, 12 feet in breadth by 40 feet in length, the second course of 20-inch stone, some 6 inches less in dimension, thence battiring of 7 feet breadth by 20 feet in length to the bridge seat. The foundation of the centre pier consists of four caissons of best sheet iron about forty feet long and fourteen feet in diameter, placed within cribs and sunk and scribed to the rock, 35 feet below low water, the sand being dredged out and the cavity filled with concrete to the top of caissons and within 8 feet of low water, whence the regular timber and stone foundation just described. The foundation of the piers are thoroughly rip-rapped beyond possibility of accident from any change in the bed of the river by washing. The foundation of pier No. 1, situated on the west bank of the river, 30 feet from the water edge, was formed by driving sheet piling, tongued and grooved, 20 feet below surface, enclosing a space of 30x40 feet, in the excavation of which the abutment was built. The opposite shore abutment, on the island, has a precisely similar foundation. The distance from first to second pier is 250 feet, thence 181 feet to third or pivot pier, thence 181 feet to pier No. 4, thence 250 feet to pier 5, then two spans of 200 feet to No. 7, thence 11 spans of 157 feet, and concluding with a span of 200 feet, to the island on the east shore.

The pivot is 362 feet in length, with a 30-foot turn-table operated by stationary steam power, supported by the main pier, and its ends when open rest on an equidistant outside pier above and below, the upper one of which is protected by an immense ice-breaker. When the pivot is opened, the space on each side of centre pier is 160 feet in the clear. The superstructure is 15 feet wide, accommodating a single track at an elevation of 32 feet above low water, and of 12 feet above the highest known water, as prescribed by the Act of Congress.

The main bridge is connected with the east bank proper by an embankment across the island of 600 feet in length, elevated to grade, thence by a trestle bridge of 400 feet across Wood's slough, thence by 500 feet more embankment, thence over the bay by an iron drawbridge of the Bollman Truss 525 feet long, comprising 6 spans, and with foundations and piers of same character as those in the river. A side track on a heavy embankment, commencing on Chestnut street and extending 1800 feet with a curve, connects the grand crossing with the main track of the C. B. & Q., and T. W. & W. roads, on the east side, while a similar embankment of about three-fourths of a mile, completes the grand and unbroken connection with the H. & St. Jo. R. R. on the western bank of the river.

This gigantic enterprise was completed in October, 1868, and thus with the subsequent completion of the great Pacific Railroad, affords an unbroken route by rail from the Atlantic to the Pacific coast; giving Quincy advantages and facilities enjoyed by no interior city of the Union.

The cost of this grand structure was as follows:

Main Bridge	$1,150,625
Bay Bridge	165,690
Embankments	149,755
Protecting Shores	33,930
Total,	$1,500,000

While many of our leading citizens by constant agitation and untiring efforts did much to secure to Quincy this great work, we must not omit to award due credit to the management of the three great lines of railroad centering here, who displayed such liberality and energy in its construction, and thus served the double purpose of advancing their own interests and those of our flourishing city.

HENRY F. JOSEPH RICKER, ESQ., BANKER.

OR "MEN OF MARK" IN QUINCY.

There are few, if any of our citizens, who struggled more persistently or successfuly in Quincy than Henry F. Joseph Ricker, from the time of his arrival here to the present day. None made a more humble start in life, and none have achieved greater comparative wealth and prominence.

Born in Germany, in 1822, he emigrated to this country with his parents in 1839, arriving at New Orleans in December of that year. Remaining there but a few months, he proceeded to St. Louis, where he also tarried a short time, and then continued up the river to Quincy. Arriving here on the 4th day of March, 1840, he obtained employment as an ordinaay laborer from John Wood, Sr., and thus assisted his father to pay for two lots he had purchased from that gentleman.

We next find him clerking in a grocery store under the Quincy House, where he remained three years.— Subsequently he also clerked for S. & W. B. Thayer, Chas. Holmes, and Albert Dancke, until 1849, when he associated with Leopold Arntzen, and opened a dry goods and grocery store. Continuing in this for seven years with great success, he accumulated considerable means, and in 1857 embarked in the produce business. In the spring of 1858 Mr. Ricker was elected police magistrate, and re-elected in 1862. About this time he began the banking and exchange business on a small scale, also selling passage tickets to and from Europe. Shrewd and cautious, every thing he engaged in prospered, and wealth came to him surely and steadily. The Illinois banks going down about this period, he bought up considerable of what was then known as "stump tail" currency, the transaction paying him handsomely. Having the confidence of the entire community, his banking business enlarged rapidly, and in 1865, the necessity for greater facilities induced him to buy out the banking house of John Wood & Co., then located on the corner of Fifth and Maine streets. Soon after, taking in Bernard H. F. Hoene as a partner, he removed his banking house to its present site, on Hampshire street, between Fifth and Sixth, where an almost unprecedented career of success has attended the firm.

Possessed of large wealth, wielding a vast influence with the German population of our city, he has done much to develop the resources of Quincy. A man of scrupulous integrity, and untiring industry, no citizen retains the confidence and esteem of the community to a more exalted degree than Henry F. Joseph Ricker.

SAW MILL.

At present Quincy boasts of but one saw mill, within its corporate limits, but this one is a model in every respect, and capable of supplying a large quantity of timber annually to the market. This large mill is admirably located on the Bay, and is owned and operated by James Arthur & Co. This is one of the most enterprising firms in the city, and they keep their mill in active operation, nearly the entire year, supplying not only the home market, but shipping also largely to points on the various railroads diverging from Quincy. There is scarcely a kind or quality of lumber or timber known to the trade but is here turned out, and our manufacturers in other departments are thus enabled to obtain material at all times, and at the most reasonable rates. The present year Messrs. Arthur & Co. have employed at their establishment 45 hands, whose monthly pay-roll averaged $2,000, and who turned out during the year 1869, about 5,000,000 feet of lumber. $100,000 is the amount of capital employed in this enterprise.

BROOM FACTORY.

One Broom factory flourishes in our city, and its proprietor is doing an excellent business in his line.—Richard Hobart is the owner.

HON. ALEXANDER E. WHEAT,

OR "MEN OF MARK" IN QUINCY.

Around the bar of Quincy clusters many recollections of the great achievements of its members, and the memorable events to which they have been witness. Distinguished for their marked talent, many of the legal conflicts in which they have participated, have passed into the *casus celebri* of American jurisprudence. Men of giant intellects, within the dusky walls of the old court house, and beside the pine tables of less stately edifices in other sections of the state, their acute reasoning and profound logic have met as steel to steel, while the magic eloquence of their voices has on many an occasion stirred populace and jury in behalf of their clients. Beyond doubt, no body of men of equal numbers has given so many master minds to the country. Without wealth or influence, they began their career, and genial spirits as they were, made their profession a labor of love as well as necessity.

Successful has have been many of these able men, none have achieved a more deserved fame than the gifted and accomplished subject of this sketch.

A native of New York, Alexander E. Wheat passed his young days on a farm with his parents, at the same time receiving a good education. Early aspiring to the law, he entered an office, and at the age of eighteen was admitted to the bar.

Young, ardent, and devoted to his profession, he came to this city and threw his modest shingle to the breeze. Faithful to the interests of his clients, and zealous for success, prosperity dawned upon him, and he soon took rank among the foremost at the bar. In 1857, he was appointed City Attorney, and in 1862, was sent to the Legislature from Adams County, becoming a marked man in that body, although one of its youngest members. Since retiring from the Legislature, Mr. Wheat has aspired to no political honors, although repeatedly urged by his friends and fellow citizens for exalted positions.

At present a member of the City Council, and a partner in the law firm of Warren & Wheat, he ranks as one of the prominent and enterprising citizens of Quincy, notwishstanding he is still a young man. A profound thinker, stout reasoner, and eloquent pleader, Alexander E. Wheat has few superiors as a lawyer, while in the social walks of life, his unassuming manners, ready flow of language and genial qualities, are no less marked.

PRINTING.

Printing is carried on to a high state of perfection in our city, and nothing in this line can be turned out in better or more workmanlike style than is done at our printing establishments. Early in the history of Quincy a spirit of commendable rivalry began among the members of the craft, and the result has been, that constant improvement and progress has marked this department of manufactures. We have now in operation five printing establishments, all of which are managed by experienced and skillful printers, and as a natural result are meeting with success. The finest work known to the trade can be had here, and at rates below larger cities. A large amount of work is done annually by these houses, not only for Quincy, but also for a large surrounding country.

The firms now engaged in this business are:—Gilmore & Skinner; Heirs & Russell; Herald Printing Co.; Whig Printing Co.; T. M. Rogers.

They do all kinds of book, job and newspaper printing, and in every style known to first class printing houses.

HAIR WORK.

Two firms carry on the manufacture of hair work, and are doing handsomely. They are: J. C. Ottenstein and N. G. Pearsons.

C. M. POMROY, PRESIDENT 1ST NATIONAL BANK,

OR "MEN OF MARK" IN QUINCY.

The subject of this sketch has had a large share in promoting the success of Quincy, and many institutions of which she may well be proud.

C. M. Pomroy was born in Massachusetts, from which State he migrated west at an early age, and located at Cincinnati. There for a short period he engaged in selling groceries, and in 1837 came to Quincy. He at once obtained employment in the pork house of Joel Rice, and continued with this gentleman until 1843, when in connection with Geo. Bond and Jas. D. Morgan he established himself in business as one of the firm of Bond, Morgan & Co. For twenty-four years this firm operated largely in pork, and the eminent success with which its extensive business was managed is a proud tribute to the sagacity and ability of its members. He was among other prominent citizens active in founding the Quincy Savings Bank, now the First National Bank —and it is but just to say that for the unprecedented success that has attended the career of that institution, it is largely indebted to the prudence, judgment, and financial skill of C. M. Pomroy. One of its first Directors, he has followed its fortunes through every stage of its existence, having filled nearly every position within the gift of the Board, and to-day, as its efficient and able President, he can in common with all those who have been instrumental in making this institution a success, look back with pride to the career of usefulness through which it has passed, to its present pre-eminent position among the financial institutions of Quincy.

While Mr. Pomroy has thus contributed largely to the success of every firm and corporation with which he has been immediately connected, he has not been less active or efficient in promoting enterprises of a public character. Active and untiring in business, in social life he is warm, pleasant and genial, and few of Quincy's citizens carry with them as large a share of public esteem for great and generous qualities as C. M. Pomroy.

PORK PACKING.

In the matter of pork packing, Quincy has been for various reasons retrograding for several years past.— True, there has been a decided falling off in the number of hogs raised during the same time; but this of itself would not have caused so vast a discrepancy between the amount packed this season, and seasons of packing five or six years ago. The great reason undoubtedly is to be found in the direct railroad connection many localities now have with Chicago and St. Louis, that were formerly tributary to Quincy. Both those cities being leading pork markets, it is not strange that with equal railroad and transporting facilities they have succeeded in diverting a portion of our trade in this line. But while this has been the case, we have been recompensed doubly for our loss in this particular by the marked increase in our jobbing trade and manufactures.

This season, considering that money is light everywhere, and pork extremely high, our packers have done remarkably well, displaying more or less activity about their establishments all the time. Thus far in the season they have packed about 25,000 head of hogs, but as the yield is light everywhere this year, it cannot be taken as an average winter's work.

The following firms are engaged in packing this season:—A. J. F. Prevost; Adams, Sawyer & Co.; C. Kathman & Co.; C. A. Vanden Boom & Co.: H. Witte, and J. Q. Adams & Co.

These firms have all extensive packing houses and are prepared to do a large business in this line.

GEORGE ADAMS, ESQ., PORK PACKER.

OR "MEN OF MARK" IN QUINCY.

The subject of this sketch has not only at all times taken a decided interest in the commercial and social advancement of Quincy, but has contributed largely by his efforts to such a consummation.

George Adams was born in Maryland, in 1814, and there served an apprenticeship as a moulder. Coming to Quincy in 1842, in connection with his brother, Jas. Adams, and Milton E. Worrell, he established the Quincy Foundry, which was built on the site of the present Chicago, Burlington & Quincy Railroad Depot. He continued in this business until 1849, when the California gold mania spreading to Quincy, Mr. Adams, with others made the trip overland to the golden shores of the Pacific. After three years experience in the mines of California, Mr. Adams returned to Quincy, and established in connection with James Adams the firm of G. & J. Adams, buying and shipping grain, and also packing pork during the winter season. This firm was afterwards changed to Adams, Sawyer & Co., but under all circumstances, and under whatever name it has operated, it has met with flattering success, and has resulted in large profits to its members. This uninterrupted success is attributable to the cautious and able management of Mr. Adams and brother, who at all times directed the affairs of the firm. Mr. Adams is now the senior member of the firm of J. Q. Adams & Co., engaged in the same line, and doing an extensive business.

Devoting himself assiduously to his business at all times, he has also given largely of his time to forward public enterprises—and within the last year has by his efforts done much towards the success of the Quincy, Missouri & Pacific Railroad, of which he is now one of the Directors, and a most ardent friend.

A thorough gentleman in every acceptation of the term, and one who has been a substantial friend of the religious and educational institutions of Quincy, Mr. Adams is the peer of any of our citizens, in the esteem and admiration of the public.

RECTIFIERS.

In addition to having here two extensive distilleries, we have also a number of rectifying establishments, which are managed by experienced and reliable firms. They do an extensive business in rectifying and purifying liquors, and employ a large amount of capital in the business. These rectifying establishments are attached to the wholesale liquor houses of the city, and the liquors manufactured thus go to supply the demand from the city and also the adjacent points in Illinois, Missouri and Iowa. The following are the firms now engaged in this line:—

Adamy & Levi; S. Berger & Co.; W. Karp: R. W. Nance & Co.; John Altmix & Bro.; F. W. Hackmann; John Meyer & Co.; Sengen, Willi & Co.

SODA FACTORIES.

Two factories for the manufacture of soda are in operation here, and turn out a very excellent quality of the same. The firms are:—Durholt & Co., and Boschulte & Knauf.

In this business capital is employed to the amount of $18,000.

JUDGE THOMAS J. MITCHELL,

OR "MEN OF MARK" IN QUINCY.

Thomas J. Mitchell, present Judge of the County Court of Adams County, was born in Cincinnati, Ohio, in 1831. As early as 1835 his parents came to Quincy, and near here young Mitchell passed his boyhood on a farm. Arriving at maturity he embarked in merchandizing, which he pursued successfully until the breaking out of the war in 1861, when he entered the army as a private in the 3d Missouri Cavalry. He was not destined to remain long in a subordinate position however, and we soon find him 1st Lieutenant, then Captain, and finally Major of his regiment. Possessed in a large degree of all those qualities of head and heart that won all with whom he came in contact, Maj. Mitchell in addition to being the idol of his regiment, became at once one of the most popular officers of the army. Devoted to the cause in which he was engaged, he was ever active and faithful in the discharge of his duties. With the exception of being captured at Charlotte Bluff, Mo., in a cavalry charge, he passed through the war unharmed, and retired in 1865 with an enviable reputation as a gallant and humane officer.

Returning to Quincy the same year, he was nominated by the Republican party for County Judge, and although the county is strongly democratic, was elected on his great personal popularity. In 1869, his term having expired, he was re-nominated, and although herculean efforts were made to defeat him, his personal popularity again triumphed, and he continues for another term of four years, as County Judge, in which position his uniform kindness, thorough integrity, and faithful discharge of duties, have won for him the highest encomiums.

FURNITURE.

In no department of manufactures have Quincy mechanics achieved greater success than in the manufacture of furniture. For years we have manufactured extensively in this line, and the furniture turned out at our factories has met with a ready sale in all the surrounding states. Many of the firms now engaged in this branch have been at it for a long period, and while they have made it pay, they have also given universal satisfaction to their patrons. The very best material for this kind of work is obtained here in abundance, and with a large force of excellent mechanics, under experienced management, is all that is necessary to insure success.

The following firms are now engaged in the manufacture of furniture:—F. W. Jansen & Son; F. Duker; Elrott & Jochem; Schutte & Co.; F. Senger; and Henry A. Vanden Boom & Co.

These firms employ 85 hands, and turn out annually $193,600 worth of furniture. The capital invested amounts to $83,000.

ORGANS.

Recently Messrs. Witney & Holmes embarked here in the manufacture of organs, at which they are having decided success. Their instruments are of excellent make, and in tone and finish will compare with those of eastern manufacture. They have already built up an extensive trade.

WM. STEINWEDELL, LEADING MERCHANT,

OR "MEN OF MARK" IN QUINCY.

While much has been accomplished for our city by the shrewd and energetic men who came here in early days from the eastern and middle states, it must not be forgotten that the foreign element has contributed vastly to the prosperity and advancement of Quincy.— German and Irish citizens have been not only active, but also prominent in every department of art and trade, and have by their thrift and enterprise, added wealth and power to our city.

Prominent among the German citizens of Quincy, on account of his thorough business qualifications, and also for the influence he wields, stands William Steinwedell, Esq., of the firm of Bertschinger & Steinwedell, leading hardware and iron merchants. Born in the city of Hanover, Germany, in 1827, he had scarcely passed the age of maturity when he resolved to cross the Atlantic, and in the broad expanse of the new world and the new republic battle for success and prosperity. Arriving in this country in 1849, having had previous experience in the hardware business, he at once obtained employment in this line as a clerk. He did not long content himself as the employee of others, but in 1851 we find him established in the same trade for himself, as a member of the same firm of which he is to-day an active and honorable member. Managed shrewdly and cautiously, yet with a liberal degree of enterprise, success has attended this firm from the outset, and to it we are indebted for many reforms in the hardware trade of Quincy, among which may be cited that of making the first direct importations from Europe to our city. At present the firm is doing a splendid business, and is a credit to Quincy.

A prominent and influential member of the Republican party, in 1862 he received the nomination for Mayor of Quincy, but the city being strongly democratic he was defeated. However, his aspirations are not of a political but of a business and social character; and while in the former he has made his mark as a sagacious and successful merchant, he is not less eminent in social circles for his rare accomplishments and genial qualities.

FRUIT AND PICKLE FACTORY.

Within the past few years Quincy has spread into such metropolitan proportions that a great many enterprises that were previously uncalled for have sprung up in our midst, and met with decided success. Among these may be cited the fruit and pickle factory started only a year or more ago, and which is now doing business on an extensive scale. Fruits and pickles of all kinds are put up at this establishment in a style that is not surpassed in the east; and the product of this house will bear comparison with goods from the oldest and most famous establishments in the country. A large section of western country is now being supplied by this firm.

ROPE AND TWINE.

Two establishments are now engaged in the manufacture of rope, twine &c., and employ during the year, on an average some twenty hands. They are owned and conducted by skillful and industrious mechanics, who do excellent work at moderate rates. The firms are:—B. H. Goodno; J. H. Wavering & Co.

The capital invested in this line amounts to $14,400.

M. JACOBS, MERCHANT,

OR "MEN OF MARK" IN QUINCY.

Among the Hebrew population of our city are many who have aided largely in the development and progress of Quincy. Many of our leading and most enterprising business men come from their ranks, and of this number is the subject of this sketch.

M. Jacobs, Esq., was born in Prussia, in 1828, and emigrated to America in 1844. He at once embarked in business in New York, commencing in the manufacture of hats and caps. He remained in New York but one year, when he proceeded to St. Louis, and there followed the same line of manufacturing. He soon gave this up and opened a dry goods house, which he conducted until 1847, when he came to Quincy and opened a clothing house. From then until now he has continued successfully in this department of trade in our city, his career having been an honorable and upright one throughout. In 1864, the citizens of the Second Ward recognizing his value as a man, and appreciating his integrity, elected Mr. Jacobs to represent them in the City Council, where he served them ably and efficiently.

A man possessed of thorough business qualifications, and full of enterprise, Mr. Jacobs is both a valuable and influential citizen.

BOOK BINDERS.

Quincy boasts at present three book binderies, where experienced and competent workmen turn out jobs not to be excelled anywhere for style and use. One of these binderies is not to be excelled in facilities and arrangements for turning out work by any in the State. All work in this line for many miles around is sent to Quincy binderies, and there is no question but what satisfaction follows. The firms are:—Herald Printing Co.; C. Eberhard; G. Hermann.

BOOTS AND SHOES.

We have in this line no extensive factories, although there is little doubt but boots and shoes could be manufactured to advantage in Quincy on an extensive scale. Some forty small establishments, where from two to seven hands are employed do remarkably well, and are yearly having additions of new firms to their number.

LOUIS BUDDEE, ESQ., LEADING MERCHANT,

OR "MEN OF MARK" IN QUINCY.

For her great prestige as a wholesale market, and the vast jobbing trade that has centered here in the past few years, Quincy is indebted in a large measure to the subject of this sketch. His sagacity and foresight first induced our merchants to branch out in the wholesale line, and his untiring industry and energy have been potent in sustaining this department of our commerce, and placing it on a permanent basis.

A native of Berlin, Prussia, Louis Buddee received his business education in the store of his father, one of the oldest houses in Berlin, and subsequently managed the business of the firm for a period of ten years. In 1848, when the people of Schleswig-Holstein called for aid to resist the encroachments upon their freedom by the Danes, he, with a number of other young men, equipped himself, and responded to the call. After several severe battles, victory perched upon their banners, and he then removed to Frankfort, where he compiled the statistics of the commerce of that city, for the use of the committee on commerce of the National Congress. The following spring, in company with several members of the National Congress, he went to Manheim, in the Grand Duchy of Baden, assisted in organizing a corps of volunteers, and was appointed to command a battalion of the revolutionary army. After the defeat of the people, he went with the remnant of his corps to Switzerland, and from there started for New York, where he arrived in October, 1849. Proceeding to St. Louis in the following summer, he at once obtained employment as commercial traveler for a wholesale house, and in this capacity first visited Quincy. Continuing with the St. Louis house several years, during that time he made a number of friends in our city, and having confidence in the future of Quincy, in 1854 he located here, purchasing the grocery and confectionery business of Emil Kull. Enlarging the business, and meeting with decided success, in 1856 he bought the Mauzey building, on the north side of the Square, and built an addition, which made it the largest store edifice in Quincy. Here he first commenced the wholesale business, but labored under many disadvantages. The success of Quincy as a metropolitan city was then a doubtful question with many of our merchants and citizens. Keokuk was looming up, and many were disposed to look upon that as the great wholesale market above St. Louis. Not so with Mr. Buddee. Ever confident that a brilliant future awaited our city, he struggled on with herculean strength, determined to build here a wholesale and jobbing mart that would compete successfully with St. Louis and Chicago. He soon induced country merchants to come here for their supplies; but still there was a want of variety in the wholesale department, and there was a want of encouragement for those who sought our city as a base of supplies. Laboring under these disadvantages, and the crisis of 1857 coming on, in 1858 Mr. Buddee was forced to retire from business. Still confident, however, of his ability to succeed here, in 1861 he induced Geo. and F. Meyer to embark in business in this city, and in partnership with them, started the first *exclusive* wholesale grocery house in Quincy. Success crowned this final effort, and prosperity attended the firm. In 1868 Geo. Meyer retired from the firm to visit Europe, and the firm now became Buddee & Meyer. The present year, in order to supply the great demand made upon Quincy for groceries, and with a view to giving it a wholesale house worthy so thriving and prosperous a city, Messrs. Buddee & Meyer consolidated with W. S. Warfield, and under the firm name of Buddee, Warfield & Meyer opened their present colossal grocery establishment in the magnificent new block recently erected by Robert S. Benneson, Esq. Here they have one of the best arranged stores in the west, equal in size and stock to any in Chicago or St. Louis, and employing twelve hands and two teams constantly.

Such has been the career of Quincy's pioneer in the wholesale trade, and who, after reviewing it, but will say that Mr. Buddee has richly earned the prosperity that has attended him, and the house of which he is the worthy head, the past few years. Who can predict the future that awaits the new firm of Buddee, Warfield & Meyer? All men of energy, enterprise, and ability, there are no bounds to the trade that must flow into them, and no limit to the extent of their future prosperity.

CONFECTIONERS.

In the manufacture of candies, confectionery, &c., four firms are engaged, and do an extensive business. They give employment to a large number of hands, and with the product of their establishments supply a large region of country. The candies and confectionery from these establishments are as pure and palatable as any that is made, and is supplied to the trade as low if not lower than eastern goods.

The firms now engaged in this line are:—Brown Bros.; W. Buehrer; Duckworth & Bugbee, and O. W. Gallup. They manufacture annually about $182,000 worth of confectioneries.

MARBLE WORKS.

Three firms do an extensive business in this line, and have large forces of men at work constantly. Our cemeteries show their taste and skill to splendid advantage, and mark them as accomplished workmen. But they have not stopped here, for these shops have turned out work that has astonished even our own citizens, by its beauty of design and faithful execution.

H. B. Volk; W. M. Robertson, and W. H. Green & Co. are engaged in this line at present. They employ on an average 28 hands.

R. W. GARDNER, LEADING MANUFACTURER

OR "MEN OF MARK" IN QUINCY.

We have spoken elsewhere of the achievements of Quincy genius in the field of invention, and come now to one who in this line has won a national if not a world-wide fame.

Robert W. Gardner, the present head of the firm of Gardner & Robertson, is a native of England, having been born in London, in 1832. He remained there only until he was seven years of age, when he removed to Scotland, where he was admitted to the Edinburgh "School of Designs," an institution conducted by the government for the purpose of educating the youth of the country in science and mechanism. Only a certain number were admitted to the institution, and these contributed a specified sum to its support. While here although a mere youth, his mechanical and inventive genius asserted itself, and he became a marked student in the school.

After receiving a thorough education, he resolved to cross the Atlantic and visit the United States. In 1849 he arrived in New York, but remaining only a short time, continued west to Illinois, locating at Rushville, and obtaining employment as a farm hand. Here he also taught school during the winter months. Passing two years in this locality, he concluded to return to Scotland to pass the remainder of his days. Recrossing the Atlantic in 1851, he returned to Scotland, and on attending the World's Fair held that year, his mind underwent a change, and he resolved to revisit the United States, which he did in a few months, again locating at Rushville as a school teacher. Soon after he came to Quincy, and engaged with Edward Turner to learn the trade of machinist. Continuing with him a little over a year, he removed to Alton, Ill., and engaged as foreman of a machine shop there. Remaining at the last named place only two years, he returned to Quincy, and associating with him Henry Mitchell, bought the old Turner machine shop, and engaged in the manufacture of steam engines and general machinery, under the firm name of Gardner & Mitchell. Subsequently they bought the Union Machine Shop, on Fifth street, and took into the firm a third partner in the person of Mr. Mitchell's brother. From the beginning, however, Mr. Gardner remained at the head of the firm, and in 1860, after various changes, he associated with him Mr. John Robertson, his present partner, since which time the firm has remained Gardner & Robertson, and passed through a career of unprecedented prosperity. In 1865 the firm built their present model machine shop for the purpose of manufacturing the celebrated "Gardner's Improved Compensation Governor."

This invention of Mr. Gardner's, which has become famous wherever steam is employed as a motive power, was first patented by him in 1860, after having experimented two years to make it more perfect. He first improved it December 27th, 1864, and had it re-issued September 5th, 1865. In November of the same year, he still further perfected it, and since then the demand for them has been so constant and increasing, that some thirty mechanics have been employed in their manufacture. They are now to be found in every state and territory in the Union, and also throughout the Canadas, and are acknowledged everywhere to be the superior of every invention of the kind in use.

In 1867, Messrs. Gardener & Robertson opened the first machinists' and manufacturers' supply store, and in 1869 enlarged the same considerably. This year they also purchased the extensive hardware and iron store of Charles E. Allen, and consolidating the business of both houses into one, are conducting the same successfully in the last named house, on Maine street, where with their thorough knowledge of the wants of the trade, and their practical familiarity with the business, a career of prosperity undoubtedly awaits them.

In addition to his efforts as a mechanic and inventor Mr. Gardner has also been prominent for his services in behalf of the social advancement of our city, and few men have labored more assiduously than him to elevate the morals and improve the religious status of Quincy.

CHAIRS.

Two extensive chair factories are now in operation and meeting with fair success. They turn out work of a superior style and finish, and have little difficulty in disposing of the same. The firms operating the establishments are :—F. C. Westermann, and H. Laake & Co.

ENGRAVING.

Three firms do the engraving for the city, and as they are all experts at the work, satisfaction is rendered. The firms are: John Hobrecker; H. Hulseman, and Ottman & Folger.

MATCH FACTORIES.

Among new enterprises recently started here is the manufacture of matches, in which Von X. Widenbauer and John Stuckman are successfully engaged.

Capt. Michael Piggott, Post Master,

OR "MEN OF MARK" IN QUINCY.

Among those who gave their time and services to the nation during the late war, none devoted themselves with more ardor and heroism to the cause of the Union, or retired from the army with a better record for fidelity and valor, than the veteran whose name heads this page.

Captain Michael Piggott, present Post Master of Quincy, was born in Ireland, in 1834, and emigrated to this country with his parents in 1841, settling in St. Louis, Mo. His parents being in indigent circumstances, when quite a boy young Piggott obtained employment as cabin boy on one of our Mississippi river steamers, and by his labors not only relieved his parents from the burden of his own support, but contributed materially to their aid and comfort from his scanty wages.— In 1850, young Piggott, then only sixteen years old retired from the river, and with commendable foresight apprenticed himself to a bricklayer, to learn that trade, that he might have something permanent upon which to rely in the future. In the spring of 1854, he removed to Quincy, and began life here a young man of twenty, with a clear head and good habits, but without even a common school education. Realizing the disadvantages under which he labored for want of an education, he at once resolved to supply that deficiency, and with a determination peculiar to the man, he at once commenced the work of educating himself. While following the business of a contractor, erecting buildings, &c., he obtained books and took his first lessons in self education, learning the alphabet, and then to spell, read and write. This accomplished the path of life grew brighter before him, and he unfortunately determined to enlarge his business. and at once contracted to erect the Hess House, now the Adams House. Mr. Hess failing, he received for his work on this building almost nothing, and lost all that he had saved in the previous four years.

At the breaking out of the war in 1861, he enlisted in the "Burge Sharpshooters" as a private. Like most of volunteers he was little versed in the art of war, but by applying himself assiduously he soon acquired a knowledge of the tactics, and was detailed to drill his comrades. Before leaving for the field of action he was promoted to Second Lieutenant, and shortly after taking the field to First Lieutenant. At the siege of Donelson he was made Captain, and served as Provost Marshal under Gen. Dodge, of Danville, Miss, in 1862. His first term of service expiring in 1864, he re-enlisted with his company in that year, and received the unanimous vote of his company for captain for the second term. With his company Captain Piggott followed the fortunes of his regiment through all its engagements, from North Missouri, to Resaca, Georgia. At the last named place he lost his leg, on the 14th of May, 1864, but continued in the service until January 21st, 1865.

Returning to Quincy, Capt. Piggott devoted himself to the laudable object of educating himself. With this object in view he purchased a scholarship in the Bryant & Stratton Commercial College, and attended two months. He soon after received the appointment of Deputy United States Assessor, but resigned this position and secured an appointment as messenger in the House of Representatives at Washington.

Upon the election of President Grant, through his individual efforts, and as a reward for his services in the cause of the Union' he received the appointment of Post Master of Quincy, which position he now fills.

An ardent republican in politics, Capt. Piggott was nominated by that party for Circuit Clerk in 1866, but the county being strongly democratic, he was defeated at the election. In his present position as Post Master Capt. Piggott has administered the affairs of the office with ability and success, rendering entire satisfaction to Democrats and Republicans alike. An industrious and faithful officer, and a thorough gentleman, no better selection for Post Master of the "Gem City" could have been made.

TANNERY.

We have one tannery in operation in our city, which turns out a superior quality of leather, and bids fair to become at no distant day one of the leading manufacturing establishments of Quincy. C. A. Furche is the proprietor and manager.

HOOP SKIRT MANUFACTURERS.

We have two firms engaged in the manufacture of hoop skirts. They manufacture first-class goods, and are meeting with splendid encouragement.

The firms are D. Gross, and A. Heyman.

HORSE COLLARS.

Three firms make the manufacture of horse collars a specialty, and do a large business in that line.

The firms are S. L. Taylor; Hickey & Woodside, and A. Loher.

A. J. F. PREVOST, ESQ., PORK PACKER.

OR, "MEN OF MARK" IN QUINCY.

The subject of the present sketch has for a long term of years ranked as one of the active and enterprising men of Quincy.

A. J. F. Prevost is a native of New York, but passed only a brief portion of his life in the Empire State, his parents removing with him to Illinois when he was but twelve years old. In 1835 he located in Brown County, and commenced life as a clerk in the store of R. H. Hurlbut, at Mt. Sterling, although then only fourteen years old. At the age of twenty, he had so commended himself to Mr. Hurlbut by his faithful attention to business and strict integrity, that he was admitted as a partner in the establishment. He continued at this for a time, when he removed to Morgan County, and there tried farming for five years. At the expiration of that time, returning to Mt. Sterling, he again embraced merchandizing, and in connection therewith packed pork on a moderate scale. In 1859 Mr. Prevost removed to Quincy, and commenced pork packing on an extensive scale. He has continued uninterruptedly at the business to this day, and is at present the largest packer in the city, the product of his house this season being half of all the pork packed.

A man of easy and affable manners, kind, and generous almost to a fault, few citizens of Quincy enjoy the popularity of Mr. Prevost, and none are more eminently entitled to it.

F. H. ALDRICH, Esq., COMMISSION MERCHANT,

OR "MEN OF MARK" IN QUINCY.

Among the young men of Quincy who have succeeded by their own exertions, in placing themselves on the road to prosperity, and who have been prominent and active in behalf of our thriving city, none take rank before the subject of this sketch.

F. H. Aldrich is a native not only of the State of Illinois, but also of the County of Adams, having been born within four miles of the Court House, on the 5th of October, 1836. His parents were among the first settlers of this section of the State, but being poor, when quite a youth, he found it necessary to obtain employment, in order to support not only himself, but also to assist his parents. Securing a situation as clerk on one of the Mississippi steamers, he retained it for five years, giving unbounded satisfaction to his employers and the public. Retiring from the river, Mr. Aldrich embarked in the commission business, also acting as steamboat agent. In this he has been eminently successful, but owes his success to the indomitable energy and determination with which he has adhered to it, and the judgment and ability he has displayed in its management. Faithful to those who have entrusted business to his care, he has made the commission business a success in Quincy, after repeated failures by others, and now finds it comparatively easy to make it profitable. For a number of years agent of the Northern Line Packet Company, he has rendered them valuable service, and to-day his place could scarcely be filled by this Company, out of our entire population. Elected Alderman in 1867, on his personal popularity, he filled the position with credit to himself and satisfaction to his constituents.

Among the youngest of Quincy's business men, Mr. Aldrich is the equal of any of her citizens in business sagacity and judgment, and a brilliant future is open to him.

BLACKSMITHS.

We have a number of firms that are engaged in horse shoeing, blacksmithing, &c. They employ more or less mechanics, and in most instances manufacture wagons, plows and agricultural implements in connection with their regular work.

The firms engaged in this line of work are:—W. Arning; T. Beatty; J. Bickelhaupt; Bolinger & Grussenmeyer; Brinkkoeter & Benhof; Edward Cassidy; Fulls & Craig; Geo. Goodapple; L. O. Hartung; W. Herlemann; G. Jackson; H. Knapheide; Koenig & Weiler; J. Longres; T. Molony; H. Nolkemper; L. Otten; Ridder & Ruth; J. Ruffio; Shefer & Ledig; L. Schmitt; A. Schwieters; C. C. Slack; E. Sturbahn; Sweeny & Co.; A. Vanfleet; Wenzel & Keiser.

GUNSMITHS.

Three gunsmiths do the work in this line, principally repairing, but also occasionally manufacturing fine guns. They are:—F. Bader; P. Eger, and F. Tobias.

COLONEL M. M. BANE,

OR "MEN OF MARK" IN QUINCY.

The subject of this sketch is one who rendered valuable service to the nation in the protracted struggle from 1861 to 1865.

Col. M. M. Bane, was born in Athens County, Ohio, in 1825, and commenced life a poor boy. Succeeding in obtaining an education, however, at the age of twenty-one he entered Sterling Medical College, at Columbus, Ohio, where he graduated in 1844, and removed to Payson, Ill. Here he continued at his profession, and taking an active part in politics was elected to the Legislature of the State in 1860.

Serving a term in the Legislature, he returned to Payson and resumed the practice of medicine, at which he continued until the breaking out of the rebellion, when he took an active part in raising the 50th regiment Illinois infantry, of which he was commissioned Colonel. This position he held for three years, participating in the siege and capture of Forts Henry and Donelson, and also the battle of Shiloh, in which last he lost his right arm, and received a gun-shot wound in the left side. At this time Col. Bane was in command of the 3d Brigade, 16th Army Corps, which command he retained for upwards of two years.

After the battle of Shiloh the serious nature of his wounds necessitated his return to Quincy, where he remained until 1862, when he again entered the field, being assigned command at Corinth, Miss., and was active in garrisoning that post during the siege of Vicksburg. In 1863, he was ordered to Pulaski, Tenn., where he commanded his old brigade, which was engaged for some time in rebuilding the Nashville & Alabama Railroad. His old regiment receiving a furlough as veterans, in 1864, he returned with them to Quincy, after which they again resumed the field, and participated with Sherman in the famous march to the sea.— In 1864, he was assigned command at Rome, Georgia, which position he held until July of the same year, when he was appointed Assistant Special Agent of the Treasury, in charge of abandoned property in Georgia. Resigning in May, 1865, he spent the following winter at Harvard Law College, and in 1866 was appointed United States Internal Revenue Assessor for the 4th District of Illinois. This position he filled until 1869, when he received an appointment as United States Internal Revenue Detective, which however he resigned the same year.

It may be truly said that Col. Bane served his country well and faithfully in the hour of her extremity, and in addition to his services as a gallant and able officer sacrificed much in the cause. Gifted and accomplished, shrewd and sagacious, he ranks as an influential leader of the Republican party in Illinois, and is destined in the future to prominence and distinction in the political arena.

COOPERS.

Where there is annually such a demand for cooperage as in Quincy, a large force of mechanics are necessarily kept busy to supply the same. The following firms manufacture largely in this line, turning out flour, whisky and beer barrels to supply the trade, of which a vast quantity are used:—J. Abbe, J. Boettle, L. Breithaupt, L. Detler, H. Feld, A. Hilbing, L. Hoffmann, Hunsaker & Beebe, F. Ihringer, M. Kaltenbach, B. H. Klimper, J. H. Kollmeier, H Kraemer, J. Kriegshauser, L. Lambur, L. Lambur, jr., G. D. Landwehr, J. G. Leo & Co., W. F. Lee, E. D. Lohmeyer, H. Lohmeyer, E. McFarland, F. Michael, H. Michael, M. Neuer, H. Noll, H. Richter, J. C. Roberts, W. Schachtsick, G. Schafer, J. B. Schroder, B. Schumacher, J. Stegemann, C. Stille, W. Stremme, G. Tieben, H. Volkeri, J. Voots, sr., H. H. Wesken, G. H. Wilpers, J. Winking.

In this line employment is given to a large number of hands, while as a branch of our manufactures it is highly important.

BASKETS.

W. Heinemeyer conducts the only basket factory in the city, but manufactures on a small scale.

N. D. MUNSON, Assist. Supt. C. B. & Q. R. R.,

OR "MEN OF MARK" IN QUINCY.

There are none whose names appear in this work who in so short a period have accomplished so much for Quincy as N. D. Munson, Assistant Superintendent Chicago, Burlington & Quincy Railroad.

N. D. Munson was born in Vermont, in which state his father carried on an extensive iron manufacturing establishment, in which when not attending school, he passed his early days, and until he arrived at maturity. Resolving then to make a tour of observation he came west, and after posting himself as to its condition and prospects, returned to his native state, where he embarked in the dry goods business. In the fall of 1854 he again visited the west, this time going into the dry goods business at Painesville, Ohio. In 1856 he went to Chicago, and accepted a position as check clerk of the Michigan Southern R. R., which position he left to accept that of shipping clerk on the Michigan Central R. R. Leaving Chicago in 1857, he proceeded to Burlington, Iowa, where he engaged in the transfer business for a brief period. Returning to Chicago, he accepted the agency of the Union Despatch Line, which he resigned in 1858, to accept the freight agency of the

C. B. & Q. R. R. at this point. In 1860 he removed to St. Joseph, Mo., as agent for the Hannibal & St. Joseph R. R. In 1861 he again returned to Chicago, and engaged in the grain business, from which he retired in 1862 to accept the agency of the Great Western R. R. at Keokuk. This position he yielded in 1864, upon his appointment as Assistant Superintendent C. B. & Q. R. R. at Quincy.

During his residence in our city as the representative of this great railroad corporation, Mr. Munson has instituted reforms and improvements, whose value to Quincy can scarcely be estimated.

A thorough railroad man, and understanding the wants of the road and its patrons, he has ever been prompt to supply such accommodations and facilities as were demanded. Few men could have rendered such universal satisfaction to the public, and none could have guarded more jealously the interests of the C. B. & Q., than N. D. Munson.

Unostentatious and reserved, but pleasant and affable, he directs and superintends the vast interests of his company centered here with clock-work ease and regularity, and during his residence among us has made a community of friends.

TIN AND COPPER WORKERS.

Several extensive establishments for the manufacture of articles of tin and copper ware are in operation here, and employ a large number of mechanics. The work from these establishments is of the most superior quality, and will compare with the work of the most famous eastern shops.

The firms manufacturing in this branch are:—Comstock, Castle & Co., G. J. Cottrell, H. C. Dasbach, F. Fischer, Grant & Fisher, H. Heeb, F. Herritt, J. Kriegshauser, W. Meyers, C. Ochsner, J. L. Pfau, sr., H. Randall, Rearick, Ritter & Co., H. Rensch, J. P. H. Royston, C. H. Scheipering, B. Schupp, L. D. White, B. H. T. Wirmer, C. G. Wurst.

SOAP, CANDLES, &c.

One large factory supplies the demand for soap, candles &c., and manufactures extensively in this line. The product of this establishment is of a superior quality, and finds a ready sale in other markets than our own.

F. Flachs & Co. are the proprietors of the same, and they are displaying an enterprise in the business which must in future be rewarded with handsome returns.

WM. G. EWING, PROSECUTING ATTORNEY.

OR "MEN OF MARK" IN QUINCY.

We have had occasion elsewhere to speak of several of the eminent men of the Quincy bar, but most of those were veterans in that distinguished body, who have passed the major portion of the three-score and ten allotted to this life in the traces. We come now to one, whose career though brilliant, is not threaded with the silver lines of age.

William G. Ewing is a native of McLean county, Illinois, where he was born May 11th, 1839. He was educated at the Illinois Wesleyan University, where he supported himself by teaching during vacations. Studying law with Hon. Robert S. Williams, at Bloomington, he was admitted to the bar in October, 1861. Practicing law in Woodford county for a short time, in 1863 he came to Quincy, and commenced the struggle of life in earnest, almost a stranger in a strange land. Studiously devoting himself to his profession, and assiduously watching the interests of his clients, he soon commended himself to the public, and was in 1866 elected City Attorney. In August of the same year the City Council appointed him Superintendent of Public Schools. Both of these positions he filled with credit to himself and satisfaction to the citizens of Quincy, and in 1867, he was re-elected City Attorney. In 1868 he received another mark of public approbation, being elected Prosecuting Attorney for the district comprising Adams and Hancock counties, which position he still retains.

Although yet in the very spring-time of life, Mr. Ewing has already made his mark as a lawyer. A profound thinker, solid reasoner and powerful speaker he has in many of the celebrated cases tried at our court displayed legal ability that marks his star as one destined to a worthy place in that constellation of brilliant minds who have made Illinois the scene of their great achievements, and of whom but few remain.

MERCHANT TAILORING.

Quincy is not behind the age in the manufacture of clothing, and she can boast of several model establishments devoted to this line of work. Here are kept constantly on hand large stocks of imported and domestic goods, which are made up to order in a style of beauty and workmanship, not surpassed in the large cities of the east.

The following are the firms:—James A. Parker, J. P. Bert, C. Heidenrich, J. Templeton, J. A. Allen, Brand & Lubert, Fechter & Kipp, Haerle & Notter, T. Holtkamp, H. Meyer, Powers & Finlay, M. Rau, A. H. Schroeder, G. Worth, H. Wulfmeyer.

PHOTOGRAPHERS.

Several handsomely furnished and excellently managed art galleries flourish in our city, and every style of the photographic art, executed by skillful artists of whom there are a number employed in Quincy.

These art rooms are owned and operated by the following firms:—Mrs. W. A. Reed, J. T. Bradshaw, J. Sanftleben, Wright & Buford, D. L. Harrison, J. E. Harvey, L. N. Howard, and A. M. Warner.

COL. J. B. CAHILL, COLLECTOR INT. REVENUE,

OR "MEN OF MARK" IN QUINCY.

Although the subject of this sketch has resided but briefly in Quincy, he is still thoroughly identified with our city and its prosperity. Prior to taking up his resdence among us Col. Cahill was well known to many of our citizens on account of his connection with the 16th regiment Illinois volunteers, in which was a Quincy company, and with which he served through the war, commanding the regiment for two years of that period.

Col. James B. Cahill, was born at Utica, N. Y., July 21st, 1838, where he remained until he arrived at the age of twenty, when he removed to Hancock County, Illinois. Here he was located, pursuing the study of law, when the war broke out in 1861, and he resolved to give his services to the cause of the Union. Enlisting as a private soldier in the 16th Illinois regiment, he proceeded with it to the scene of action, and remained with it to the close of the war, commanding it the last two years of its service. While in the army he was promoted through the various grades of Lieutenant, Captain and Major to Lieutenant-Colonel, which is ample evidence of his ability and gallantry as an officer.

Settling in Warsaw at the close of the war, he remained there until President Grant's inauguration, when he received the appointment of Internal Revenue Collector for the 4th District of Illinois. President Grant could not have selected a more faithful and efficient officer, as subsequent experience has proven; Col. Cahill having since assuming the position managed its affairs with signal ability and integrity.

CIGARS.

A large business in the manufacture of cigars is done annually in Quincy, and several large establishments are employed in this line. The very best of tobacco is secured by these firms, and the quality of the cigars made by them is such that they meet with a ready sale.

The following firms are engaged in this branch :— W. Kochanowski; H. Aldag; Heinz & Co.; E. Achtermann; W. A. Bader; Bernstein & Co.; H. Cohen; D. Ehlers; E. Hanke; J. W. Hartung; A. H. Heine; Heine & Hummer; A. B. Hiltz; Jackson, Keuser & Co.; S. Kingsbaker & Co.; P. Mueller; F. Sleumer.

These firms manufactured during the twelve months just closed 1,280,236 cigars.

WATCH MAKERS AND JEWELERS.

Our watchmakers and jewelers have at all times taken front rank for enterprise in their business, and while their stores have been at all times temples of beauty, they have also employed skillful and experienced jewelers to do the work of their patrons.

The following are the firms in this branch :—W. H. Gage, J. W. Brown, George Mitchell, J. S. Rosenthal & Co., J. F. Andrews, A. Basse, jr., J. Brockschmidt, B. R. Hemming, F. Hofling, H. Hulsman, R. Waldin.

COL. CHARLES H. MORTON, COUNTY CLERK,

OR "MEN OF MARK" IN QUINCY.

None of those who entered the army from Quincy attained greater prominence for fidelity and devotion to the cause they espoused, than Colonel Charles H. Morton.

Col. Morton is one of the old residents of Quincy, coming here as early as 1835 with his parents. Arriving at maturity he studied medicine in Quincy, and followed that profession until 1862, when he entered the army as Major of the 84th regiment Illinois infantry. With this regiment he passed through all the campaigns of the Army of the Cumberland in Kentucky, Tennessee, Alabama and Georgia. In November, 1863 he was captured at Chickamauga, but on his release again took the field, and subsequently commanded the 84th at the capture of Atlanta, and the battle of Nashville, being promoted to Lieutenant-Colonel and brevet Colonel for gallant and meritorious services on the last named occasions. Returning home at the close of the war, Col. Morton having been a zealous and active Republican, was nominated for County Clerk by that party in 1865. The county being hopelessly democratic, it was not imagined that he would be elected, but at the polls his personal popularity overbalanced political odds, and he was triumphant. Serving four years he was renominated, and redoubled exertions were made to defeat him, but to no purpose, he being again the successful candidate.

As County Clerk, his present position, Col. Morton has been industrious, faithful and efficient, which, added to his genial and social qualities as a man, made him a formidable candidate before the people.

BAKERS.

In the manufacture of bread, crackers &c., we have a large amount of capital employed. Bread of a superior quality is made here, but is almost entirely for local consumption. In the manufacture of crackers there is still greater activity, and a heavy demand from abroad is annually supplied. The trade in this particular is constantly increasing, and our large establishments are kept busy the year round filling orders.

The following firms are engaged in this branch of manufactures:—Brown Bros., Duckworth & Bugbee, O. W. Gallup, M. Jarrett, W. Buehrer, H. A. Althoff, C. Bummann, Deuerlein & Kohler, G. Kirschner, H. H. Krins, J. Manegold, C. Meien, J. C. Roller, Thuer & Hellhake, J. B. Wheeler, A. Wichmann, H. Boekenhoff.

They employ 98 hands, and a capital of $210,000.

BAKING POWDER.

D. C. Clinton has recently embarked in the manufacture of baking powder, and is meeting with fair success.

COL. K. K. JONES,

OR, "MEN OF MARK" IN QUINCY.

Although the subject of this sketch resides onside of Quincy, he has been prominently identified with its prosperity for the past fifteen years, and his interests are now so identified with those of our city that he is emphatically one of her citizens.

K. K. Jones is a son of the late William Jones of Chicago, who at the time of his death was one of its wealthiest and most influential citizens. Born in Chatauqua County, N. Y., when but an infant his parents removed to Buffalo, where they remained until he was ten years of age, when they went to Chicago, his father having first visited Chicago in 1831.

On his thirteenth birthday he entered a printing office, and at eighteen associating with him Dr. J. S. Beach, established a weekly paper called the *Gem of the Prairie*. This modest weekly which then enlightened the pioneers of Chicago, was the foundation upon which has since been built the great "*Tribune*" of that city, one of the most profitable newspaper enterprises of the nineteenth century.

In 1848, disposing of his interest in the "*Gem*," Mr. Jones removed to Manitowoc, Wis., and began business on a small scale. He found this decidedly a wooden country—lumber, saw logs, shingles and cord wood being legal tender. By close attention to business, and hard work, he however succeeded in making it profitable, and in 1851 commenced vessel building, continuing at it more or less for several years.

In 1857 Mr. Jones came to Quincy, and the following spring settled on his farm known as the "Pines," near this city. Here he continued farming successfully for years, having one of the best stocked, most admirably arranged, and most valuable farms in Illinois. In 1866 he purchased his present suburban residence known as the "Wedgelands," a magnificent country place with a handsome and commodious dwelling and beautiful grounds surrounding the same.

The past summer Col. Jones purchased the controlling interest in the magnificent new Opera House here, and adding some improvements, has gone to work to make it a benefit as well as ornament to Quincy.

Possessed of indomitable enery, and unbounced enterprise, few men are better calculated to advance a city than Col. K. K. Jones, and none are more ready to give time and money for such a purpose. Warm and impulsive, there is no medium with him. Whatever he advocates he gives a whole-souled, earnest support at all times. A friend of railroads and public enterprises calculated to enrich and develop a country, he has actively encouraged them. An ardent republican, he upholds the principles of that party with all his might, and is a zealous and influential member of the same.

BAGS.

Two firms operate extensive factories for the manufacture of bags in this city, and in addition to supplying the local demand, also ship largely to points up and down the river, and on the various railroads. An extensive trade in this line has been built up in the last few years by the energy and enterprise of those engaged in the business. West of here goods in this line are rarely found bearing any other than Quincy brands, and the trade is almost entirely monopolized by this city. This is attributable to the fact that our manufacturers have facilities for turning out better work and at lower rates, than any western city.

The firms engaged in this line are:—Morphy & Charles, and W. M. Avise. They employ 23 hands and a capital of $43,000.

MISCELLANEOUS.

Below we give a list of firms engaged in the unimportant branches of manufactures here, which employ but a small amount of capital and give employment to but few hands.

WHITE BEER—P. Antweiler, sr.

BELL HANGERS—A. Cross, and H. Randall.

BLEACHERS—C. Verniaud, and Jo. Woillard.

CABINET MAKERS—A. L. Proescher & Co., J. Braun, H. Brinkmann, F. Hellstern, H. Kanngieszer, J. Kiefer, J. C. Reincker, C. Steren, C. Stevens, J. H. Timmermann & Co., P. Volm.

CARPET WEAVERS—J. Evans, C. Gehm, E. J. Green, E. P. Lake, K. Storck, and L. Weber.

WOOD CARVERS—John Hobrecker, G. W. Althans.

Cord and Tassel Manufacturer—J. Mohr.

Dyers and Scourers—C. Goll, H. Worden, A. T. Adams.

File Cutter—W. Dienstuhl.

Box and Measure Factory—John Potter.

Furnace Builder—C. Ochsner.

Furrier—G. J. Laage.

Gas Fitters and Plumbers—J. R. Bunting & Co., P. Lally, Missouri Portable Coal Gas Co.

Glass and Glazed Sash—Bimson, Menke & Co.

Grinders of Cutlery—J. Blocher, D. Grosch, G. Langguth, B. Woll.

Locksmiths—H. Randall, and E. Sien.

Patent Medicine—A. J. Kalb.

Metal Worker—J. A. Schneider.

Millwrights—J. C. Hartley, and S. F. Ross.

Mustard Manufacturers—W. Hoffmann, and Sengen, Willi & Co.

Picture Frames—W. Brown & Co., and J. Hass.

Pottery—C. Brenner.

Railroad Excavating Machine—B. T. Stowell.

Regalia Manufacturer—M. W. Newton.

Roofing—Smith & Hughes, and O. C. Steele.

Saddletree Factory—Vogel & Vosmer.

Sash Supporter Manufacturer—J. D. Simmons & Co.

Shirt Maker—J. Grafftey.

Silver Platers—Ottmann & Folger.

Trunk Factory—H. Thomasmeyer.

Turner in Wood—G. Langguth.

Undertakers—S. M. Bartlett, A. L. Proescher, H. Brinkmann, F. Duker, and H. Kanngieszer.

Vinegar Factories—J. Wich, and Sengen, Willi & Co.

Upholsterers—C. Haubach, C. Mewes, and H. Zimmermann.

F. W. MEYER, LEADING MERCHANT,

OR "MEN OF MARK" IN QUINCY.

While Quincy has been the scene of operations of many successful merchants, it is doubtful whether any of them achieved prominence and success as early in life as the subject of this notice.

F. W. Meyer, is a native of Germany, where he was born in the village of Berne, Oldenburg, in 1836. Emigrating with his parents to the United States in 1848, he first located at Milwaukee. From there he proceeded to St. Louis in 1851, and clerked for two years. Returning to Wisconsin, he worked about his father's saw mill for two years, but the climate not agreeing with him he again went to St. Louis and obtained employment as shipping clerk and salesman in a wholesale grocery house.

In 1861 he came to Quincy, and in company with Louis Buddee and G. F. Meyer established the first exclusive wholesale grocery house in the city. His health failing he retired from this firm in 1867, and visited a number of the celebrated springs of Germany, when he returned, and associating with Louis Buddee formed the firm of Buddee & Meyer, which has since done an enormous business in groceries. The past fall this firm and W. S. Warfield consolidated their houses under the firm name of Buddee, Warfield & Meyer, and took possession of the commodious store rooms in Benneson's new block, which they have filled with a ponderous stock of groceries. They are now doing an extensive wholesale trade in groceries, and have a stock which in quantity and quality is unsurpassed in the west.

That Mr. Meyer has by his thorough business tact and knowledge done much to bring this firm to its preeminent position is well known, and that it is destined to renewed success and prosperity under its present able and sagacious management cannot be doubted.

MERCANTILE.

WHOLESALE DRY GOODS AND NOTIONS.

First in importance, perhaps, of all trades in the city is the Wholesale Dry Goods and Notions, in which line we have houses that can boast of a trade surpassed by few establishments in the East. New York has her Stewarts and Claflins, whose energy and enterprise have won for them the title of Merchant Princes of the Continent; but we, here in a city of 40,000 inhabitants, far removed from the seaboard, have our Lesem and Johnson, whose business tact and liberality bid fair to place them high in the list of leading merchants of the country. Already we have houses whose sales verge on to two million dollars annually. Few St. Louis or Chicago houses can say as much.

Our Jobbers in Notions and Fancy Goods are meeting with equal success, and also making large annual sales.

Their goods are bought in the East where men are kept to watch the fluctuations of the market and advantage themselves of all opportunities for favorable purchases. They have equal opportunities in freights with Chicago and St. Louis, expenses of business, rents,

&c., are less, and as a consequence merchants trade to better advantage here than in either of the above cities. The sales in Dry Goods and Notions by wholesale houses the past year averaged $268,333 per month, or $3,220,000 for the year.

The following firms are engaged in these lines. W. H. Johnson & Co., S. J. Lesem Bro. & Co., Chauncy Ladd & Co., Byerly & Brittingham, Joseph & Nelke, Ladd & Talcott, J. Meyer & Co., H. Roberts, J. Putman.

ROBERT TILLSON, ESQ.,

OR "MEN OF MARK" IN QUINCY.

The subject of this sketch is one of the few who having witnessed Quincy's early struggles as a frontier settlement has also the privilege of viewing her as a metropolitan city, with an extensive trade, important manufacturing interests, and untold commercial facilities.

Robert Tillson was born August 12th, 1800, in Massachusetts, and at the age of twenty-one emigrated west, locating at first at Hillsboro, Illinois. Remaining there until 1827, he proceeded to St. Louis, and with Charles Holmes as a partner engaged in the mercantile business. In 1828, loading their entire stock of goods on a keel boat they brought them to Quincy, and started the first general store ever established here, their place of business being a log cabin on the north-east corner of the public square. In 1829 they built and occupied the first frame building erected here. This was on the south-west corner of the square, the present site of Mr. Tillson's handsome block of stores. In 1831, Mr. Tillson bought out the interest of his partner, and continued the business alone for several years. While conducting this business Mr. Tillson was also post master, serving for twelve years, decidedly the longest term of any post master in the history of Quincy. In 1838, he represented the 2d Ward in the City Council, and then as at all times was zealous in promoting the city's prosperity.

Early turning his attention to real estate, Mr. Tillson secured at comparatively trifling figures some of the most desirable property in Quincy, much of which he still owns. This he has improved with splendid business structures, and has been second to none in enterprise and public spirit.

One of the earliest settlers here, perhaps the best testimonial to his character is that in a residence of forty-two years his energy and integrity have stood unimpeached, while to-day he retains the confidence and esteem of the entire community.

WHOLESALE GROCERY TRADE.

No branch of business in Quincy has flourished more successfully or increased with greater rapidity than the Wholesale Grocery Trade. A few years only have elapsed since the Wholesale Grocery establishments of our city numbered only two, whose annual sales did not aggregate a quarter of a million dollars. The statistics of this year's business shows the aggregate sales of Groceries by our Wholesale Houses, to have averaged $230,000 per month or $2,760,000 for the year just closing; nor is it strange that the sales have become so large. There is no good reason why Quincy should not supply a large region of Western Illinois, North Missouri, Southern Iowa and Kansas with Groceries. Our merchants purchase their stocks in the East to as good advantage as Chicago and St. Louis houses; freights to Quincy are as cheap as to either of the aboved named places; expenses incident to business are much smaller here, and our merchants are consequently able to sell for a smaller margin, and therefore, to the advantage of merchants in the interior. To merchants West of the Mississippi, Quincy presents many advantages as a Wholesale mart. The item of freight deserves attention, and the amount saved (in that particular) to merchants in the West purchasing here instead of Chicago or St. Louis, is by no means inconsiderable. No market affords finer Groceries, a better variety, or more honorable and liberal dealers than Quincy.

The following firms are engaged in this trade, Buddee, Warfield & Meyer, S. E. Seger, Bartlett & Co., Thos. Austin & Co., D. W. Miller, Wheeler, Andrews & Co., and Meyer & Kespohl.

HON. JACKSON GRIMSHAW,

OR, "MEN OF MARK" IN QUINCY.

Of all the gifted men whose master intellects have shed an effulgent glow of greatness upon the bar of Quincy, none have displayed more marked ability than the subject of this sketch.

Hon. Jackson Grimshaw is a native of Pennsylvania, having been born in Philadelphia, in 1823. There while attending school he devoted himself to the study of engineering, and at the age of seventeen was employed as a civil engineer on the New York & Erie Railroad. He continued at this for five years, when he removed to Pike County, Illinois, and there began the practice of law. Meeting with success in this, he continued to practice uninterruptedly in Pike County for fourteen years, at the expiration of which time he removed to Quincy, and here associated with the late Archibald Williams, With Judge Williams he continued as a partner until death dissolved the firm, and robbed our bar of one of its brightest ornaments. The history of the firm of Williams & Grimshaw during its existence, forms a bright page in Illinois jurisprudence, the firm figuring in many of the celebrated cases then before our State Courts, and successfully contending with the greatest legal talent of the country.

While a member of this firm in 1856, Mr. Grimshaw was nominated by the Republican party for Congress from the Quincy district, but the democracy being in the ascendant he met with defeat.

Since then he has been urged at various times for exalted political position, but has steadily declined to enter the political arena as a candidate. On the death of Judge Williams he continued the practice of law, associating with him Mr. John H. Williams, son of his former partner. In 1865, being appointed Collector of Internal Revenue for the 4th district of Illinois by President Lincoln, he partially retired from the practice of law, but on the expiration of his term of office in 1869, again resumed the practice of the same.

Full of life and energy, possessed of ripe judgment and rare ability, Col. Grimshaw is just in the noon-day of success at the bar, with years of usefulness and eminence before him. A man of warm impulses and genial manners, his friends are to be found in every section of the State, while in Quincy none outrank him in public esteem.

WHOLESALE HARDWARE AND IRON.

So constant has been the growth of manufactures in the West, and so increasing is the demand for material, tools, implements and cutlery, that it has required no little effort upon the part of our Hardware and Iron Merchants to keep pace with the onward march of trade, yet, notwithstanding all this our Jobbers and Dealers have been found equal to the emergency, and their supplies of Hardware and Iron have been, at all times, equal to the heavy demand. Not only have they carried the requisite quantity, but their stocks have been so satisfactory and advantageous to interior merchants that trade in this line has marked a steady increase, showing that the inducements offered here have had the desired result of attracting business to this mart. St. Louis and Chicago find it up hill work to compete with the enterprising dealers of Quincy for the trade of Missouri and the country adjacent to the Mississippi river, above and below this point. This year will undoubtedly mark a new era in the Hardware and Iron business, as trade has increased to such dimensions that competition is crowding in, new houses are being established, enterprise is more active, and goods are being marked lower and lower to prepare for the opening year. Come what may the year 1870 promises to be an active one in this department of business and our merchants are straining their energies for the work. The sales for the year just closed foot up a handsome total, but another year, we doubt not, will show a marked advance.

Sales per month average $64,000 or $768,000 for the year. The firms are Bertschinger & Steinewedell, Gardner & Robertson, Geo. Ant. Roberts, J. T. Lemley, S. Jonas, G. J. Cottrell, and H. & J. H. Tenk.

WHOLESALE DRUGS.

The supply of drugs, medicines &c., carried by the jobbers of Quincy is unequaled in quantity and quality by any city of its size in the Union, and we do not hesitate to say that we have houses whose stocks equal the most extensive establishments of Chicago or St. Louis. Their stocks are not only large, but are justified by the demand, and the amount of goods shipped from this market indicates a healthy and growing trade.— Our jobbers possess the energy, enterprise and capital to win success, and druggists and dealers in Illinois, Missouri and Iowa who have not tried this market will do well to give this city a call and satisfy themselves of the many advantages it offers over other points. We deem it unnecessary to further urge the claims of Quincy drug houses to the trade adjacent and west of here, as we are well satisfied that the quality of their goods, and the prices at which they sell, are the advertising cards upon which they principally rely for patronage. The sales of drugs during the year averaged $108,750 per month, and aggregate $1,305,000 for the year.

The following are the firms engaged in the trade:— Montgomery & Co., Rogers & Malone, Brink & Thieneman, W. H. Alexander & Co., Schultheis Bros., and Geo. A. Miller.

ALDO SOMMER, LEADING MERCHANT,

OR "MEN OF MARK" IN QUINCY.

Of the many German citizens who have achieved success and accumulated wealth by their industry and energy in Quincy, none contributed more largely to advance the city in commerce, wealth and power than Aldo Sommer, Esq., now of the extensive wholesale drug house of Montgomery & Co.

Emigrating to this country in 1849, then only eighteen years of age, after considerable experience in business elsewhere, he came to Quincy in 1857, and engaged in the drug business. He commenced as one of the firm of F. Flachs & Co., and in 1860 succeeded to the exclusive control of the business. In 1864, in connection with Wm. Metz, he established the firm of Sommer & Metz, and opened an extensive wholesale and retail drug house. Selling out this business in 1869, the same year he entered the firm of Montgomery & Co., wholesale druggists, as a partner. This firm carries a stock equal in quantity and quality to any St. Louis or Chicago houses, and does an extensive business. Besides his experience in the drug business Mr. Sommer has been engaged in the nursery business since 1862, as one of the firm of Hargis & Sommer. He has also contributed largely to the material wealth and beauty of Quincy by erecting many handsome business structures and comfortable residences, and has in every sense of the word proven a valuable and enterprising citizen.

WHOLESALE BOOTS AND SHOES.

The trade in boots and shoes at this point is extensive, and large stocks are sold and shipped annually. Our boot and shoe establishments are of the very first order, carrying large amounts of goods, and conducted by men whom a lifetime's experience has thoroughly posted in the trade. Energetic, enterprising and liberal, we venture nothing in saying that they sell at as low rates as any merchants in the west. Interior merchants are fast realizing the advantage of supplying themselves from this mart, and a comparison of Quincy's bills with those of Chicago or St. Louis, will convince the most skeptical that we hold over both the above cities as a base of supply for Western Illinois, North Missouri, Southern Iowa and Kansas. It requires little consideration to discover the advantages we possess in freights, rents, expenses of business, &c., over these points.

Sales of boots and shoes for 1869, averaged $80,000 per month, or $960,000 for the year. The firms engaged in this trade are:—Kingsbury Bros., A. S. Coburn, Chas. Brown, jr., & Co., F. Wilms, Wentworth & Co., Rosenheim & Stern, and I. Benjamin.

A. B. KINGSBURY, LEADING MERCHANT.

OR, "MEN OF MARK" IN QUINCY.

Prominent among those who early embarked in the wholesale trade in Quincy, and labored to establish it upon a permanent basis, stands the subject of this sketch.

Born in Massachusetts, at the age of twenty-one Mr. Kingsbury migrated west and located in Quincy.— Here he entered the boot and shoe house of E. K. Stone, and at the expiration of three years was admitted as a member of the firm. The house was then doing a wholesale and retail business in boots and shoes, and in 1864, Mr. Kingsbury purchasing the interest of his partner, established the firm of Kingsbury Bros. Continuing at the old business and old stand until 1865, this firm then sold out, and locating in new quarters, on the west side of the square, opened an exclusive wholesale boot and shoe house. The first exclusive wholesale house in this line established in Quincy, it has been instrumental in building up the jobbing trade of our city, and has met with flattering success.

In addition to being one of the most thorough of our business men, Mr. Kingsbury is also noted for his enterprise and liberality, which with his long experience in western trade are sure guarantees of a successful career in the department in which he is engaged.

BOOKS AND STATIONERY.

The progress of civilization and the advancement of people in arts and sciences, bring with them necessarily a demand for books, papers, and periodicals, the great sources of information and the implements that perform a noble work in the culture of the human mind. It has been well said that the only solution to the social problem, is universal enlightenment, and this being the case, it speaks volumes for the character of our population to state that our numerous book and stationery houses find a sustaining element in the west "where the sun never rises." The demand for books and stationery is constant and increasing, but the supply in quantity, quality and variety has been equally large. We have a bindery turning out work equal in style and finish to any establishment in the country. The sales of books and stationery amount to $19,070 per month, or $228,840 per year.

Dayton & Arthur, O. W. Brooker, J. R. Skinner, Herald Printing Co., F. E. Doyen, G. A. Miller, E. Long, Woodruff & Pfeiffer, and Benning & Oenning are engaged in this trade.

S. P. BARTLETT, LEADING MERCHANT.

OR, "MEN OF MARK" IN QUINCY.

The subject of this sketch, although one of the youngest of our business men, ranks as one of the shrewdest and most sagacious merchants of Quincy, on account of his thorough business tact, untiring energy and wonderful enterprise.

S. P. Bartlett is a native of Quincy, being born here in 1840. At an early age his business career began, and at seventeen we find him clerking in the store of J. M. Smith. Subsequently he was also employed in the same capacity at different periods by James Lowe, S. Lesem, and S. A. Brittingham. In 1861, tiring of working for others, he resolved to embark for himself, and opened a warehouse for the purchase and sale of grain. Finding this rather discouraging he speedily retired from the field, doing very little until 1865, when he was employed in the Provost Marshal's office. In 1866 he again resumed business for himself, buying out the grocery house of S. A. Brittingham, on Hampshire street. From that time to this success has attended him in every form, and his house has prospered to a degree almost unprecedented. The past year, so vastly had his business increased, that he found it necessary to obtain more commodious quarters, and with this object in view he took possession last August of the magnificent store erected by Mr. McBane, on Hampshire street, between Third and Fourth. Here, associating with him Walter N. Colburn, he opened the extensive house of Bartlett & Co., which has since achieved a reputation for enterprise and activity, seldom if ever enjoyed by any Quincy firm.

Both men of thorough business qualifications and sterling integrity, with the enterprise for which they are proverbial, the firm of Bartlett & Co. is destined to a long term of uninterrupted prosperity.

WHOLESALE HATS AND CAPS.

In the hat and cap trade we have both dealers and manufacturers with stocks unsurpassed by any city.— Furs, gloves and umbrellas are embraced in this line, and fine stocks are supplied to the city and country trade, and at the very lowest rates. Merchants in this department have equal advantages with others, and do a handsome business.

Sales amount to $27,500 per month, or $330,000 for the year. Wholesale firms are :—G. J. Laage, Wood Bros., and Reis Bros.

WHOLESALE MILLINERY.

Reports of sales in millinery goods show an aggregate of $128,000 for the year. Large stocks in this line are held by dealers here, and interior dealers consult their interests by patronizing them.

The following firms are engaged in this line of business:—W. C. Gallaway & Co., J. Merrilies, and M. Jackson.

LOUIS MILLER, PROPRIETOR TREMONT HOUSE,

OR "MEN OF MARK" IN QUINCY.

While Quincy has had many successful hotel keepers, and has supplied one or two large cities with their most popular landlords, she has never had one who combined in a greater degree the elements for a successful landlord than the subject of this brief sketch.

Louis Miller, present proprietor of the famous Tremont House in this city, is a native of Holland, from whence he emigrated in 1853 to America, locating at St. Charles, Mo., and establishing a house for the sale of millinery goods. Attending closely to business, and displaying a liberal degree of enterprise, he soon succeeded in building up a fine trade, which he however gave up in 1860, in order to open on a more extensive scale in Quincy. Here his success was more flattering than ever, and he continued prosperously in his old business until 1864, when he purchased the furniture and secured a lease of the Tremont House.

Since taking possession of this hotel, Mr. Miller has succeeded by his enterprise and energy in making it one of the first houses in the west. Aiming at all times to accommodate and please, his house is made a home of luxury and ease for the traveling public, and few hotel men enjoy as enviable a reputation, or can count as many friends as Louis Miller. At present the "Tremont" is one of the famous institutions of our State, made so by his genial manners, untiring energy and unbounded enterprise.

WHOLESALE CHINA, GLASS, &c.

In this, as in other departments of business, we have live, active and thorough business men. One or two import directly from Europe, and every variety of goods known to their line of trade can be purchased here cheaper than in Chicago. In fact Chicago and St. Louis bills are discounted 5 per cent., and if interior merchants ask for more liberal traders than these they are difficult to please. Sales per month, $11,500, aggregate per year, $138,000.

The firms in this line are:—O. B. Barton, Gerry & Macfall, H. Ridder & Co., H. Rensch, C. Goodman & Bro., and A Gatchell.

AGRICULTURAL IMPLEMENTS.

In addition to manufacturing agricultural implements on a large scale, we have several firms here who sell extensively machines and implements manufactured elsewhere. These firms are T. Butterworth, Pope & Baldwin, J. M. Smith, and G. W. Moulton & Co.

There sales for 1869 amounted to $430,000.

WM. B. ANDREWS, LEADING MERCHANT,

OR "MEN OF MARK" IN QUINCY.

The subject of this sketch during his residence in Quincy has passed through an uninterrupted career of success in business.

William B. Andrews is a native of Connecticut, where he was born in 1830. At the age of twenty-one he emigrated to California, and there engaged in the mercantile and mining business. After three years experience on the Pacific slope he returned to his native State in 1855, and soon after entered the wholesale dry goods house of Geo. Bliss & Co., New York City, as a salesman. Remaining with this firm two years, at the expiration of that time he embarked in the dry goods business for himself, at his old home, Winstead, Conn. Here he continued until 1863, when he came to Quincy, and associating with him Samuel Bruckman, established the extensive dry goods house which was managed and conducted with flattering success by the firm of Bruckman & Andrews.

This firm closing out its business in the spring of 1866, in the following July Mr. Andrews associating with him Mr. J. F. Wheeler, under the firm name of Wheeler & Andrews, engaged extensively in the wholesale and retail grocery business. The past year they took in a third partner in the person of Ed E. Manson, and the present style of the firm is Wheeler, Andrews & Co. Since its establishment this house has prospered to an extent far beyond the anticipations of the firm, and its business has annually met with a large increase.

Much of this prosperity is due to Mr. Andrews, who in addition to being one of our shrewdest and most experienced business men, has a reputation of buying to rare advantage. Already doing a heavy jobbing business, the firm is destined in this respect to rank at an early day with the exclusive wholesale houses of Quincy in the amount of goods sold.

WHOLESALE CLOTHING.

We have at this point some of the most extensive clothing houses in the west, and have merchants who have been engaged in the business here for a score of years. Liberal and active business men, they have met with merited success, and carry immense stocks with which to supply the trade. Their goods are of the best quality and sold at living prices. Sales in clothing for 1869 averaged $31,000 per month, and aggregate $372,000.

The following firms are engaged in this department of trade:—J. D. Levy, Bro. & Co., Meyer & Whitehead, M. Jacobs, J. Parkhurst, Powers & Finlay, D. Hermann, M. Rau, and Rosenheim & Stern.

WHOLESALE CARPETS.

Two firms make carpets a specialty, and keep constantly on hand large stocks in this line. All grades of goods known to the trade are sold by these houses, and they offer inducements in prices not afforded by Chicago or St. Louis.

These firms are W. H. Johnson & Co., and Bert & Hill. Their sales for 1869 aggregated $250,000.

HENRY ALLEN, LEADING MANUFACTURER,

OR, "MEN OF MARK" IN QUINCY.

While this work contains a brief record of the achievements of many of our most valuable and enterprising citizens, none whose names are mentioned take precedence for public spirit and enterprise before Henry Allen, Esq.

A native of the District of Columbia, when only twenty-two years old he embarked in the grocery trade in Quincy, locating in what was then known as the Kelly Building, the same now occupied by Dimock & Hilborn, corner 5th and Maine streets. Here he continued to do an extensive business, and in 1849 took in as a partner James T. Baker, the firm name then being Allen & Baker. In the fall of 1852, desiring to embark in a business less confining, Mr. Allen sold his interest to Mr. Baker, and engaged in purchasing, selling and shipping hay, grain &c. The same year in connection with Joseph G. Rowland and Charles Howland, he built the extensive planing mill, and sash and door factory corner 9th and Hampshire streets. This he continued to run as the senior and managing partner, until 1857, when the crisis putting a stop to improvements, he sold out his interest, and the following year associated with Messrs. H. V. Sullivan and T. Owens, in the purchase of the City Flouring Mills. Subsequently he bought out both his partners, and in 1866 sold the mill to Mr. Henry Whitmore of St. Louis. In 1867-8 he engaged successfully in pork packing, and in the latter year, with Mr. Whyers, an old employee and experienced miller, purchased the Centre Mills, which they enlarged and refitted, and where they are now actively engaged in the manufacture of flour. In 1867-8 Mr. Allen also engaged in pork packing with H. S. Osborn, Esq., but since then has confined his operations to flour.

In enterprises of a public character Mr. Allen has been among the foremost of our leading citizens, taking an active part in the building of the Opera House, Adams County Fair Grounds and Skating Rink and also in the establishment of the Quincy & St. Louis Packet Company, &c. To all of these he contributed liberally from his means, while at the same time he has also aided munificently the educational and religious interests of Quincy.

Agreeable and unassuming in his manners, straightforward and upright in business, and a polished and christian gentleman, Mr. Allen is esteemed and admired by the entire community.

COAL.

It requires but a glance at our enormous and extensive manufactories to ascertain that a large amount of coal is annually consumed here. This is brought here by the railroads entering the city from adjoining counties, and is furnished in abundance at reasonable rates.

The following firms supply the city:—Morris & Burns, J. B. Parish, and F. Kreismann. Their aggregate sales in 1869 amounted to $319,560.00.

COAL OIL.

H. A. Williamson is the only exclusive wholesale dealer in coal oil, of which he sells annually a large amount.

FISH MARKETS.

Fresh fish from the Mississippi River and tributary streams is supplied the year round by the following dealers:—G. H. Hellman, Jenks & Curtis, J. Platt & Bro., Scott & Dervine, and Scott, Jenks & Co.

COL. JOSEPH G. ROWLAND,

OR "MEN OF MARK" IN QUINCY.

The subject of this sketch in a residence of nearly twenty-four years in Quincy, has been largely instrumental in promoting its advancements.

Joseph G. Rowland was born in Wilmington, Delaware, in 1830. After receiving his education at Philadelphia, and when only sixteen years of age he migrated to Quincy, locating here in 1846. Studying medicine, he graduated in 1852, but did not devote himself to the profession, preferring to engage in manufacturing.

In 1854, in connection with Henry Allen and the late Chas. Howland, sr., he built the planing mill on Ninth and Hampshire streets, but in 1856 engaged in the real estate business, at which he continued until the breaking out of the war.

On the 20th of April, 1861, he enlisted in the three months service, and was commissioned Adjutant of the 10th regiment Illinois infantry. Re-enlisting for three years in July, 1861, he continued as adjutant of his regiment until February, 1862, when he was promoted to the position of Major. Tendering his resignation in June of the same year, pending its acceptance he was promoted to Lieutenant-Colonel, but did not remain in the service.

Returning to Quincy and resuming business, in 1868 he was elected to the City Council from the 6th Ward, and while in that body was indefatigable in his efforts to relieve the city from its financial embarassments and to introduce reforms in the municipal government. It is due to him to say that the city never had a more faithful, energetic and competent officer.

FLOUR AND FEED.

The following firms are engaged in the flour and feed business, and have commodious warehouses, where they keep a constant supply for the trade:—J. W. Bass, jr., & Co., R. C. Coles, Dennis & Bro., John G. Naylor, Dix & Ehrgott, W. H. Doyle, J. G. Lee & Co., James Purnell, O. Thom, and W. Wrightmire.

FORWARDING & COMMISSION.

We have in our city two extensive commission houses, managed by reliable and honorable business men, who annually do a large business in forwarding and selling goods shipped by river and rail.

These firms are F. H. Aldrich, and Schermerhorn & Bro.

WHOLESALE FURNITURE.

Two firms do an extensive business in this line, shipping furniture to all points west of the Mississippi river, and also into the interior of Illinois. These firms keep constantly in their mammoth ware rooms large stocks of furniture, manufactured in the most workmanlike manner, and after the most approved style. They sell cheaper than eastern houses, and hence have built up a fine trade. These firms are:—Spiegel, Thoms & Co., and F. W. Jansen & Son. Their sales for 1869 amounted to $270,000.

SAMUEL E. SEGER, LEADING MERCHANT,

OR, "MEN OF MARK" IN QUINCY.

Among the merchants of Quincy who have achieved success in business, none have labored more persistently and with greater determination than Samuel E. Seger, at present a leading wholesale grocer.

A native of New York, Mr. Seger at an early age determined to try his fortunes with the young and growing west. Arriving in Quincy in 1852, he at once obtained employment in a grocery house as clerk, and continued there until 1857, when with a small stock he embarked in the retail grocery trade. Attentive to business, prudent and industrious, it was not strange that prosperity favored him, and we soon find him in one of the largest houses of the city, with a mammoth stock of groceries, and an extensive wholesale and retail trade. This trade he retains to-day, and after a long business career in Quincy, ranks second to none of her citizens as a man of integrity and honor.

Also one of the most active and zealous of our citizens in organizing and perfecting the fire department of Quincy, he devoted time, money and labor lavishly to that laudable work.

Quiet and retired in his manners, of easy and affable address, Mr. Seger is thoroughly a business man, and finds himself in his proper element directing and managing the affairs of his extensive grocery house.

GRAIN.

The purchase and shipment of grain is a business that constantly employs a large amount of capital in Quincy. The following firms are engaged in this line: J. Q. Adams & Co., F. Bernbrock, Bernbrock & Reichl, J. Burns, jr., C. Kathmann & Co., R. Hutmacher, J. G. Lee & Co., Schermerhorn & Bro., and J. M. Wilson.

HIDES, FURS, WOOL, &c.

A number of enterprising firms are engaged here in the purchase of hides, furs, and wool, which are received and shipped in large quantities annually. In this line a great deal of enterprise has been displayed in the past few years, and the trade has grown to be an important item in our commerce.

The firms are:—Gurley, Pratt & Collins, Z. Hirsch & Co., Z. Hirsch, jr., J. Jonas & Co., C. A. Furche, E. Kling, Schott & Bro., H. Steinkamp, H. Swimmer, and G. Vassen.

WHOLESALE LEATHER.

Five establishments deal extensively in leather, supplying the local trade and also shipping to points in the interior of Illinois and west of the Mississippi. The firms are: S. L. Taylor, Boon & Tillson, Schott & Bro., C. Sellner, and A. Seyd.

GEN. B. M. PRENTISS,

OR, "MEN OF MARK" IN QUINCY.

Of those who entered the army during the late war, none figured more prominently and usefully in its early stages than Gen. B. M. Prentiss, of this city, of whom we are about to write.

Gen. Prentiss was born in Wood County, Virginia, in 1819. Migrating west from there in 1836, he located in Marion Co. Mo., and engaged in the manufacture of cordage. In the spring of 1841 he came to Quincy and established himself in the same business, being associated with his father. At this he continued until 1847, when he commenced the study of law, studying for five years. He did not practice the profession until the close of the late war.

During the Mormon excitement in this section he was in the service of the State, and at the opening of the Mexican war was appointed Adjutant of the lamented Hardin's regiment raised here, and called the 1st Illinois infantry. With this regiment he served through the entire war, returning to Quincy at its close. In April, 1861, upon the first call of President Lincoln for 75,000 troops, Gen. Prentiss at once raised a company, was elected Captain, and soon after appointed Colonel of the 10th Illinois infantry, and ordered to Cairo. The latter point was then the rendezvous for most of the western troops, and he was placed in command of the post. From there he was ordered by Gen. Fremont to Jefferson City, Mo., to take command of all north and central Missouri. Subsequently being ordered to the field by Gen. Halleck, he proceeded to Pittsburg Landing, where he arrived April 1st, and organized and took command of the Sixth Division. On the morning of the 6th his command was attacked by a superior force of the enemy, against which he contended the entire day, being overwhelmed and captured in the evening. He remained a prisoner for six months, during which time he was confined at Talledega, Selma, Madison and Libby prisons. An exchange of prisoners being effected he visited Washington, and was granted a leave of thirty days, but before its expiration was ordered to sit on the court-martial in the case of Gen. Fitz John Porter. At the close of this trial he was ordered to report to Gen Grant at Milliken's Bend, by whom he was assigned the command of the eastern district of Arkansas, with headquarters at Helena. Here on the 4th of July, 1863, he commanded the Union forces in the battle of Helena, gaining a decided victory over the enemy, whose forces were equal to four times his number. Previous to this he had been promoted for gallantry at Shiloh, and commissioned Major General.— After the battle of Helena, he however deemed it his duty to resign and return home to his family. Returning here he commenced to practice law, and has devoted himself to that profession ever since. On the 1st of April, 1869 he was appointed by President Grant

Pension Agent for the 4th District of Illnois, which position he fills at present. Although at all times evincing a generous public spirit, and manifesting an active interest in Quincy's prosperity, he has in the past year redoubled his exertions to promote her interests, having been untiring in his support of the new railroad projects started here. An influential Republican, he has been frequently urged for high political honors by his party, but has of late declined to enter the political arena as a candidate, preferring to devote himself to his profession, in which he has met with merited success.

WHOLESALE LIQUORS.

The liquor trade of Quincy is carried on with marked enterprise and energy, and no department of our wholesale business is conducted by more liberal and responsible dealers. Their stores are model establishments, filled with the best imported and domestic wines and liquors, and most of those engaged in this branch of trade being thoroughly versed in its wants, are enabled to guarantee satisfaction. This trade has grown to magnificent proportions of late, and the demand upon our merchants still increases.

The following firms are engaged in this business: — Adamy & Levi, Ira N. Malin & Son, D. W. Miller, H. Leifhelm, John Meyer & Co., R. W. Nance & Co., John Altmix & Bro., S. Berger & Co., F. W. Hackman, W. Karp, W. & A. Kolker, Sengen, Willi & Co., E. Stockle & Co., Edward Cohn & Co.

MUSICAL GOODS.

Musical goods of every description are supplied here as low as they can be purchased in the east. Pianos, melodeons, organs, violins, guitars, &c., also sheet and bound music are kept constantly on hand by our dealers, who are enterprising and liberal merchants.

The firms are: Woodruff & Pfeiffer, E. Long, R. E. Letton, and A. Sumner.

NEWTON FLAGG, ESQ.,

OR "MEN OF MARK" IN QUINCY.

In awarding credit to whom it is due, Captain Newton Flagg deserves a prominent place in this work, he having for years been identified with Quincy's prosperity, and by his time and talents, contributed largely to her progress.

Capt. Flagg is a native of Connecticut., having been born at Hartford in that State. He came to Quincy while yet in his teens, and entered the store of Levi Wells as a clerk. Subsequently he also clerked for J. T. Holmes, G. B. Dimock, and W. D. Skillman. In 1842 he purchased the book and stationery establishment of the latter, and continued in that business up to 1850, when he disposed of the same to J. R. Dayton. The same year, associating with Charles A. Savage, and I. O. Woodruff, he established the first bank in Quincy, under the firm name of Flagg & Savage. This bank continued in operation for many years. With Mr. Savage he built in 1858 the substantial and imposing block of buildings on the corner of Maine and Fifth streets, one of the finest business structures in the city.

At the breaking out of the war in 1861, Capt. Flagg was appointed Quarter Master of the post of Quincy, which position he held until its close, discharging its responsible duties with signal ability.

In November 1866, he was appointed agent and treasurer of the Quincy Railroad Bridge Company, and in that position rendered valuable service in purchasing supplies and supervising the voluminous affairs of the company, while the grand structure that now spans the river at this point was being built. On the completion of the bridge he closed up the affairs of the Company, having paid out as agent of the Company in less than two years $1,500,000.

In his career as a business man and financier, Capt. Flagg has at all times had the confidence and esteem of the entire community. A generous friend of all enterprises of an educational, charitable, and commercial character, he has given substantial evidence of his friendship, and has been foremost among those to whom Quincy is indebted for her present pre-eminence.

LUMBER, SHINGLES, LATH, &c.

The amount of lumber annually sold in Quincy is simply enormous, and instead of falling off is constantly on the increase. The past year, too, a decided advantage has been gained in the matter of shipping west. An extensive lumber yard has been established on the west bank of the river by Messrs. Bradford, McCoy & Co., and thus the toll by bridge or ferry over the Mississippi for lumber going west is avoided, and saved to the purchaser. Another advantage that we have as a lumber market is that several of our dealers have mills in the lumber regions of Wisconsin, and manufacture their own lumber, thus being enabled to sell at the very lowest rates.

The following firms are engaged in this line:—Bradford, McCoy & Co., D. D. Meriam & Son, R. McComb, Meisser & Dickhut, Geo. Neeves & Son, VanDoorn, Bro. & Co., James Arthur & Co., J. C. Blanchard & Co., H. H. Merten.

The aggregate sales of these firms for the year 1869 were—lumber 23,000,000 feet, shingles 13,000,000, and lath 7,000,000.

PAINTS, OILS AND GLASS.

This trade is supplied by two enterprising firms, who keep constantly on hand large stocks of the finest and best goods sold. The firms are Letton & Viberts and D. E. Lynds.

PAPER—FLAT, PRINT, &c.

The *Herald* Printing Company has an extensive warehouse, where a full stock of paper for newspaper and job printing offices is kept constantly on hand. This establishment supplies a large number of interior and western towns with goods in this line, and does an extensive trade.

SALT—WHOLESALE.

Large quantities of salt are annually consumed here, and it is also sold and shipped in abundance. The following firms supply the wholesale trade—H. A. Williamson, Wm. Morris & Co., and Gurley, Pratt & Co.

SEEDS—WHOLESALE.

A supply of all kinds of field and garden seeds is at all times kept in our city and they are of the purest and best sold. Pope & Baldwin and W. Eber supply the trade in this line.

SEWING MACHINES.

Five sewing machine agencies are established in our city, and most of them have model warerooms in which to exhibit and dispose of goods. A flourishing trade is carried on by most of them in supplying Quincy and the surrounding country. The firms are: M. W. Newton, A. Sumner, D. Snitjer, R. E. Letton, and E. J. Elgin.

GEORGE W. BURNS, ESQ.,

OR "MEN OF MARK" IN QUINCY.

The subject of this sketch has for years been one of the most active and enterprising citizens of Quincy.

George W. Burns was born in Maine in 1825, and migrated west with his father in 1834, settling in Quincy. From 1834 to 1849 he engaged in various occupations to earn a livelihood, a large portion of the time laboring at the hardest work. In the latter year, when the California gold fever spread to this section, he with many others proceeded to the new Eldorado, hoping of course to accumulate wealth with greater speed than was possible in the then diminutive town of Quincy.

Remaining but one year in the mines, he returned to Payson, in this county, where his father resided, and engaged in the mercantile business. In 1854, he again took up his residence in Quincy, and associated with Messrs. Bagby & Wood in building the famous Castle Mills. Here he continued until 1862, when being appointed paymaster in the army with the rank of Major, he sold his interest in the mill and started South.— While filling the duties of his position as paymaster in 1864, he was captured on Red River, Texas, and held prisoner for three months. When paroled he returned to Quincy, and has since engaged in many enterprises, vastly beneficial to our city. He was president of the association that erected the magnificent new Opera House, and is at present secretary and treasurer of the Quincy Coal Company.

A generous and genial gentleman, his business activity and integrity are only equalled by his personal popularity.

TINNERS' STOCK.

The following firms supply the demand for stock used by tinners in the manufacture of their wares:— Comstock, Castle & Co., G. J. Cottrell, L. D. White, and Rearick & Rensch.

TOBACCO LEAF.

One establishment is devoted to the sale of leaf tobacco for the manufacture of cigars. Mr. W. Kochanowski is the author of this enterprise, and is doing handsomely at it.

WHOLESALE TOBACCO, CIGARS, &c.

An extensive wholesale trade is carried on by our manufacturers and dealers in cigars, tobacco, &c.:—S. Kingsbaker & Co., W. Kochanowski, E. Hanke, A. M. Claflin, and Jackson, Keuser & Co.

WALL PAPER AND SHADES.

In this line there has been decided enterprise and the stocks held by dealers are both large and varied. All goods usually kept by first class houses in this line can be had here, and at the lowest rates. The firms are D. E. Lynds, Letton & Viberts, G. A. Miller, and I. Zimmerman.

F. W. JANSEN, LEADING MANUFACTURER,

OR, "MEN OF MARK" IN QUINCY.

The subject of this sketch is one who early embarked in manufacturing here, and who has by his industry and energy built up an extensive trade and accumulated large wealth.

F. W. Jansen is a native of Prussia, where he was born in 1815. In 1834, being then only nineteen years of age, he emigrated to this country without relatives, and located at St. Louis. Remaining there only one year and a half, in 1836 he came to Quincy, and obtained employment as a cabinet maker, with Geo. Wood. In 1838 he commenced business for himself, establishing his first cabinet shop and wareroom, both in one, on Maine street, between Sixth and Seventh, using Maine street for a lumber yard. Subsequently he removed to a frame store, which stood on the present site of Coburn's shoe store, north of the Court House, Soon after he bought his present stand two doors south of the Court House, of Joel Rice, and removed to the same.

When he first commenced business, Mr. Jansen employed only one hand, while to-day he is the head of the firm of F. W. Jansen & Son, which runs one of the largest furniture factories in the State, employing as high as sixty-five hands, and in connection with their factory, occupying one of the largest stores in the city for their warerooms.

One of the first alderman of Quincy, being elected when the city was organized, he has at all times manifested a deep interest in the progress of our city, and has liberally aided with his means in advancing her religious and educational interests.

MISCELLANEOUS.

The following are the firms engaged in the less important branches of trade.

AUCTION AND COMMISSION—Brougham & Son, H. Kohn, Pricer & Jackson.

BOOK AGENT—J. W. Marsh.

CLOCKS—Wardell & Co.

COFFEE AND SPICES—Treat & Co. and A. M. Claflin.

EUROPEAN PASSAGE AGENTS—T. T. Woodruff and H. F. J. Ricker.

FAST FREIGHT LINES—F. Bradley, W. Harvey, Schermerhorn & Bro.

TRANSFER TEAMS—J. Clements, Hall & Co., P. Henricks, and Norton & Co.

INSURANCE AGENTS—W. F. Pitney, L. H. Baker, S. P. Church, Geo. W. Foss & Son, P. C. Keller, J. J. Langdon, Penfield & Bishop, Mrs. L. H. Thompson, J. C. White, Wilson & Corey, C. H. Bull, Charles de Lescluze, Hamburgher & Lesem, B. J. Hawkes, R. H. Hurlbut, Hutton & Boam, C. H. La Beeres, J. L. Miles, E. H. Osborn, Parker & Bull, S. P. Parker, A. H. Potter, B. H. Potter, J. Rhoades, G. M. Rogers, J. C. Scroggs, C. Seeger, C. Thomas, F. Thompson, and C. Witzemann.

LADIES' FANCY GOODS—M. Flachs and H. L. Sommer.

LIGHTNING RODS—R. Ash.

LIME—A. Carroll, W. D. Meyer, H. Surmeier, M. Zimmermann, and Zipf & Gehring.

LIVERY, SALE AND EXCHANGE STABLES—J. L. Hatcher, Millard & Byington, Miller & Hughes, J. S. Agey, and Emmons & Aldrich.

MASONIC BOOKS AND GOODS—Wm. M. Avise.

MEAT MARKETS—V. Kauder, J. Lock, jr., J. M. Ballance, C. W. Braun, J. Fey, Gasser & Monsag, J. Gehring, M. Grunbaum, H. Kaiser, C. Kauder, Klarner & Lock, Klarner & Oakley, W. Lock, B. Netter, A. Oertle, J. Oertle. J. & V. Pfirman, F. Schwab & Co., K. Schwab, D. Veihl, Werneth & Barth, S. Werneth, and J. Whitbread.

NEWS DEALERS—O. W. Brooker, F. E. Doyen, Benning & Oenning, R. B. Winn, P. S. Janes.

NURSERIES—Hargis & Sommer, and J. H. Manning.

OMNIBUS LINE—Miller & Hughes.

ONE DOLLAR STORE—Hall & Bunt.

PHOTOGRAPH GOODS—E. Long.

PRODUCE AND COMMISSION—H. A. Williamson, J. W. Bass, jr., & Co., J. Burns, jr., and Bernbrock & Reichl.

REAL ESTATE—W. F. Pitney, E. H. Buckley and Son, S. P. Church, J. P. Erskine, D. Paullin, C. A. & A. E. Savage, W. E. Avise, Brougham & Son, M. B. Denman, J. B. Gilpin, Hutton & Byam, R. Jansen, L. Kingman, J. H. & J. W. McGindley, Moore & Co., J. S. Nelson, M. G. Palmer, H. T. Patten, E. Prince, O. A. Turner, and R. K. Turner.

SAND AND GRAVEL—Quincy Sand and Gravel Co.

STEAMBOAT AGENTS—F. H. Aldrich and Schermerhorn & Bro.

WOOD YARDS—T. Bimson, W. S. Chevalier, A. C. Denman, C. Gruell & McElfresh, and W. Trowbridge.

R. S. BENNESON, Ex-Mayor of Quincy.

OR, "MEN OF MARK" IN QUINCY.

Some men are born to prosperity, while others carve it out of the very desert of life, and rear an oasis of success in its midst.

Of this class is Robert S. Benneson. Born in Newcastle County, Delaware, at the age of 14 he commenced riding the mail, and continued at this four years, when he returned to his father's and learned the shoemaker's trade. He continued at this but one year, when he determined to learn the carpenter's trade. He worked at that one year in the vicinity of his home, when he went to Philadelphia, and there completed his apprenticeship. Remaining in that city for nine years, working at his trade, at the end of that time he resolved to visit the west. In 1837, he proceeded via Pittsburg to St. Louis, and thence up the river. On the arrival of the steamer at Quincy, he took a stroll through the then unpretentious town to take observations, and was so impressed with the place that he returned to the boat, ordered his baggage ashore and settled for life. His first employment was with Nathaniel Summers, who was engaged in erecting a house on the site of the present Post Office. He continued at the carpenter trade up to 1840, when he associated with him Wm. Dickhut, and engaged in the lumber trade. This firm continued for sixteen years, and upon its dissolution he formed a co-partnership with John W. Corill and N. D. Benneson, under the firm name of Benneson & Co., which lasted for four years, when Mr. Benneson withdrew, and engaged in buying and improving real estate. At this he has been eminently successful, and the past year completed a block of stores that in beauty of design, durability of structure, and admirable adaptation to business, are unsurpassed anywhere. During his residence in Quincy, Mr. Benneson has filled many positions of trust and honor, being twice elected alderman, once mayor, and also President of the Quincy Gas Light & Coke Co. He is at present Director of the First National Bank, a position he has held from its organization, and fills the same position in the Gas Company, and Quincy, Alton & St. Louis Railroad.

There is no citizen of Quincy who has labored more zealously, and given more generously to promote the moral, social and commercial welfare of our city, and none who rank higher in public esteem.

HOTELS.

Quincy is particularly fortunate in having a number of first class hotels, kept in the very best style, and managed by enterprising landlords. In this line the Tremont House, Quincy House, and Wilson House are models that are equal in every respect to the best houses in the country. Besides these there are a number of smaller houses and all together offer abundant accommodation for the traveling public.

The following is the list of hotels: Tremont House, Quincy House, Wilson House, Adams House, Sherman House, Virginia House, Ballard House, Magnolia House, Oehmen House, Union Farmers' Home, Armbruster's Hotel, Broadway House, European House, Farmers' Home, Farmers' House, Fifth Ward House, Gem City Hotel, Kentucky House, Maine Street Union House, Mississippi House, Pennsylvania House, Prairie House, Railroad House, Sengen House, Stadt Dresden, Star Hotel, Union House, Waterford House.

RESTAURANTS—F. Ralph, James Wilson, A. Steidel, Fourquet & Lehnerts.

BILLIARD ROOMS—James Furlong, Quincy House, Tremont House, James Wilson, Buchheit & Ruter.

E. K. STONE, RETIRED MERCHANT,

OR "MEN OF MARK" IN QUINCY.

The subject of this sketch was one of the early merchants of Quincy, and has been identified with the prosperity of our city for a long period.

E. K. Stone is a native of Massachusests, being born at Grafton, in that State, in 1818. He remained there until he was 20 years of age, when he migrated west, locating at Alton, Illinois. Remaining but one year at Alton, in 1839 he came to Quincy, and obtained employment as salesman in the store of Joseph Haywood. Shortly after he established himself in the boot and shoe business one door east of the Quincy House, but subsequently removed to the west side of the square.— On the completion of the building now occupied by Brown & Pope, he opened there the first wholesale boot and shoe store in our city, associating with him Mr. A. B. Kingsbury, the firm name being E. K. Stone & Co. In 1866 he sold his interest in the firm and retired from business.

Mr. Stone has at all times been an active and useful citizen. He served one term as alderman, and has ever manifested a decided interest in Quincy's progress.

PROFESSIONAL.

ARCHITECTS—R. Bunce, L. F. Lakey, C. Petri, and G. Raby.

ARTISTS—P. Prescott, R. W. Conrad, D. Hely, F. C. Richter, and J. Wahlert.

ATTORNEYS AT LAW—Arntzen & Richardson, Benneson & Janes, Browning & Bushnell, E. H. Buckley, J. M. Cyrus, Duff & Tyrer, Emmons, Butz & Prentiss, W. G. Ewing, Goodwin & Davis, Jackson Grimshaw, E. B. Hamilton, U. H. Keath, J. H. & J. W. McGindley, E. Prince, G. J. Richardson, Scoggan & McCann, Skinner & Marsh, J. C. Thompson, R. K. Turner, Warren & Wheat, Wheat & Marcy, J. H. Williams, Henry Asbury, G. W. Fogg, F. S. Giddings, C. Greely, H. H. Jansen, R. L. Miller, I. M. Moore, H. T. Patten, A. Wheat, jr.

CIVIL ENGINEERS—B. I. Chatten, E. R. Chatten, Peter Smith, Charles Petri, L. T. Sides.

DENTISTS—S. M. Sturgiss, E. D. Helms, DeCrow Bros., F. N. Elliott, Lewis & Smith, C. F. Konantz, S. & P. Hubbard.

PROFESSORS OF MUSIC—J. E. Hoefer, A. Bernhardt, G. H. Littlejohn, and J. F. Grosh.

PHYSICIANS—M. F. Bassett, W. W. Elgin, G. W. Edson, S. H. Hess, F. W. J. Rittler, Springer & Nichols,

S. A. Amery, L. H. Baker, J. W. Bartlett, M. E. Brown, J. H. Buecking, L. H. Cohen, Curtis & McMahan, J. B. Cutts, M. Doway, F. Drude, S. W. Durant, E. E. Ehmann, J. Gunther, J. N. Hummer, J. T. Kinsler, P. A. Marks, G. D. McIntyre, A. Niles, H. Oehlmann, G. Park, A. Ples, Ralston & Kendall, M. J. Roeschlaub, Schmidt & Koch, C. A. Streeter, Talcott & Brown, Torrence & Nance, W. P. Torrence, J. VanSteenbergh, L. Watson, L. H. Wilcox, Wilson & Robbins, C. A. W. Zimmermann, sr., C. A. W. Zimmermann, jr.

W. H. JOHNSON, ESQ., LEADING MERCHANT,

OR, "MEN OF MARK" IN QUINCY.

Of all the successful merchants of Quincy, none rank the subject of this sketch for sterling business worth, indomitable energy, and unbounded enterprise.

W. H. Johnson, head of the leading dry goods firm of W. H. Johnson & Co., is a native of Albany County, N. Y., where he was born in 1837. Remaining in New York until 1850, he then removed to Cincinnati, where he passed a thorough apprenticeship in the dry goods business, studying its details and becoming versed in its various phases. Commencing in the employ of others without a dollar at the age of nineteen, at twenty-three, by his tact and energy, he was enabled to establish himself in business. Remaining in Cincinnati until 1864, in that year he removed to Bloomington, Illinois, and opened there an extensive retail dry goods house, conducting it with great success until 1867.

Retiring from business in Bloomington, in 1867, associating with him Mr. F. L. Crosby, his present partner, Mr. Johnson established the two extensive wholesale and retail dry goods houses of W. H. Johnson & Co., one at Springfield and the other in this city. The Springfield house did a business the first year of $250,-

000, and the Quincy establishment $500,000, showing the experiment to have been a decided success in both cities.

With the opening of 1869 Mr Johnson secured the magnificent block of stores erected by W. B. Powers, of this city, and fitting it up in a style of elegance and taste seldom equalled in the great cities of the east, opened it with a magnificent stock of dry goods, carpets, etc., to the wholesale and retail trade. This establishment is a temple of beauty, and is managed and conducted with admirable success.

Mr. Johnson's personal appearance indicates the man —quick, energetic and systematic, he is in every sense a business man, who finds his rarest enjoyment in the routine of daily commercial transactions.

THE "PRESS."

While many agencies have been at work to advance and improve Quincy, it is indisputable that the "Press" of the city has contributed largely to her growth and prosperity. We have been peculiarly fortunate in this particular in having at the head of our city journals men of enterprise and sagacity. Ever prompt to support and advocate any measure calculated to benefit, improve, or enrich Quincy, her newspapers have been a power for good, to whom she is vastly indebted for the progress she has made in commerce, arts, and science.

The "Press" of Quincy at present comprises four journals. The oldest of these, the

QUINCY HERALD,

is now in its 36th volume, having been established in 1834. It is Democratic in politics, and wields a powerful influence in the party. Its circulation is larger than any Democratic paper in the State, outside of Chicago, and a period of prosperity has dawned upon it, that promises soon to place it in the front rank of the leading newspapers of the country. A few months since the Herald Printing Company, by whom it is published, occupied the new HERALD building, erected especially for them, and now have one of the most complete newspaper and job printing offices in the State. Austin Brooks, Esq., who has been connected with the HERALD for over a quarter of a century as proprietor and editor, is its present editor, assisted by James H. Wallin. The proprietors are Jno. P. Cadogan, A. Demaree, I G. Huffman, and H. J. Gardner, who form the Herald Printing Company.

THE QUINCY WHIG AND REPUBLICAN

Is next in age to the Quincy HERALD, having had an existence of 32 years, during which time it has faithfully and steadily fought for the best interests of Quincy. It was an influential organ of the Whig party until the demise of the latter, when it espoused the principles of the Republican party, and has been a herculean worker in both. Skillfully managed and ably edited, it is to day a leading organ of the Republican party, having a large circulation and being in a prosperous condition. It is edited by Gen. John Tillson, with P. H. Bailhache as assistant. The publishers are Maj. W. H. Bailhache and D. L. Phillips, who form the Quincy Whig Company.

Both of the above are daily morning papers.

THE EVENING JOURNAL

Is the only daily evening paper printed in English. Although it has not been long established, the JOURNAL has made itself useful, and has proven a valuable acquisition to the "Press" of Quincy. Its management has displayed commendable enterprise in its conduct, and it has taken rank as an influential journal. The past summer it also moved into new and commodious quarters, and has now one of the finest offices in the State. Independent in politics, it is devoted mainly to the local interests of Quincy and the surrounding country. T. M. Rogers and A. H. Lacy are its editors, and the former is its proprietor and manager.

In addition to the English dailies, we have the

QUINCY TRIBUNE,

published daily in German, which is well sustained by the large German element in our city. It is owned and managed by T. M. Rogers, Esq., proprietor of the EVENING JOURNAL, and performs good work in its proper sphere. Louis Korth, Esq., is the editor, and discharges the duties of the position with marked ability.

A German monthly publication, entitled

DER ERZ-DRUIDE,

now in its 5th year, is also issued by Charles Petri, Esq., who edits the same in the interests of the United Ancient Order of Druids. It is the official organ of the order. This is a neat paper, creditable alike to the publisher and the organization of which it is an exponent.

WESTERN AGRICULTURIST.

This publication, devoted to the interests of agriculture, is issued by T. Butterworth, and is ably edited and managed.

RESUME.

QUINCY HERALD............	Published by	Herald Printing Co.
QUINCY WHIG & REPUBLICAN	" "	Quincy Whig Co.
QUINCY EVENING JOURNAL....	" "	T. M. Rogers.
QUINCY TRIBUNE, (German)...	" "	T. M. Rogers.
DER ERZ-DRUIDE, (German)..	" "	Charles Petri.
WESTERN AGRICULTURIST......	" "	T. Butterworth.

JAMES ARTHUR, LEADING MANUFACTURER.

OR "MEN OF MARK" IN QUINCY.

While Quincy has many sources of wealth and power, she may rely to a great extent upon her manufacturing interests for permanent prosperity—and hence the debt she owes those, who like the subject of this sketch have struggled through years of uncertainty, to build here a manufacturing center.

Mr. Arthur emigrated west in 1835, touched at St. Louis, and then continued up the river to Galena. Returning to St. Louis, he obtained employment as clerk in a wholesale boat store. Remaining with this house two years, at the expiration of that time he established himself in the dry goods and grocery business. Retiring from this, he accepted the position of commander of a steamboat, and after continuing at this a few years came to Quincy in 1845, and established himself in the boat store business. In 1847 he embarked in pork packing, and subsequently associating with him the late Joseph E. Norwood, erected a commodious pork house on the bay. To this he devoted his time and capital until 1855, when he erected the extensive saw mill now operated and managed by him, in connection with J. A. Van Doorn, since which time he has engaged exclusively in the manufacture and sale of lumber, employing permanently some fifty hands, and running steadily almost the entire year round.

Mr. Arthur has served the city efficiently as alderman, but his achievements have been rather in the quiet walks of social life, and in his business. A man of unquestionable integrity and honor, his success in business is the result of indefatigable industry, and prudent management. Enterprising and public spirited, he has at all times manifested a deep interest in the moral and social elevation of Quincy, while his own life has been that of an unostentatious and practical christian.

BANKING INSTITUTIONS.

Quincy is well supplied with banking institutions, which afford ample facilities to her business men in the daily mutations of commerce, and through their able management encourage legitimate enterprise, and advance the city generally in wealth and importance.

THE UNION BANK OF QUINCY

Occupies one of the handsomest business structures in the city, and has every modern convenience for security and speed in the transaction of its business. It was established by a number of the solid men of Quincy and Adams County, and in its management can boast some of the most skillful of our financiers. Many of our wealthy citizens are stockholders in this institution and its directors are as follows: Henry Root, H. S. Osborn, Joseph Sibley, J. M. Earel, Aldo Sommer, E. M. Moffett, Samuel E. Seger, Wm. Charles, and Isaac Lesem. The officers are: Henry Root, Pres., H. S. Osborn, V. Pres., E. M. Moffett, Cashier, C. H. Charles, Ass. Cashier.

FIRST NATIONAL BANK OF QUINCY.

This famous institution was first established as the "Quincy Savings Bank" under the State law in 1857,

The first directors were John Wood, sr., R. S. Benneson, C. M. Pomroy, Hiram Rogers, and Elijah Gove. The officers were: E. Gove, Pres., A. C. Marsh, Sec'y, C. B. Clark, Cashier. In 1864 it merged into the First National Bank of Quincy under the same management, and has continued through a career of unprecedented prosperity. Its directors at present are: C. H. Curtis, C. M. Pomroy, O. C. Skinner, Thomas Jasper, George Bond, R. S. Benneson, F. Collins, Amos Green, Edward Wells. The officers are: C. M. Pomroy, Pres., Thomas Jasper, V. Pres., U. S. Penfield, Cashier.

Mr. Penfield has served this institution faithfully and with marked efficiency for a long term of years, and bids fair to remain its honored cashier for years to come.

MERCHANTS' AND FARMERS' NATIONAL BANK.

In 1864 the Merchants' and Farmers' National Bank of Quincy was organized, and since commencing business has proved vastly beneficial to our commercial community. Its directors are: Lorenzo Bull, N. Bushnell, C. H. Bull, O. H. Browning, and E. J. Parker. The officers are: Lorenzo Bull, Pres., N. Bushnell, V. Pres., C. H. Bull, Cashier, and E. J. Parker, Assistant Cashier.

H. F. J. RICKER & CO.'S BANKING HOUSE.

Perhaps one of the safest and most successful private banking houses in Illinois is that of Henry F. Joseph Ricker & Co. in this city. This house was established by Mr. Ricker in 1860, he having done business on a small scale previously. In 1865 he purchased the banking house of John Wood & Co., where he remained three months, when he removed to his present stand, and associating with him Bernard H. Frank Hoene, established the banking house of Henry F. Joseph Ricker & Co., one of the most successful in Quincy.

THOMAS T. WOODRUFF, BANKER.

Still another private banking house and one that has successfully operated for several years, is that of Thos. T. Woodruff. This was established by Mr. Woodruff in 1866, and has been managed liberally, but prudently.

EDWARD WELLS, ESQ.,

OR "MEN OF MARK" IN QUINCY.

One of the most successful as well as one of the most influential citizens of Quincy, is the subject of this sketch.

Edward Wells was born in Newburyport, Massachusetts, in 1813, which place he left at the age of seventeen, removing to Boston. In 1834 he left Boston for Quincy, arriving here in October of that year, after a journey of thirty-six days, the time then required to make the trip. Being a cooper, he at once obtained employment at his trade, but soon after associating with Gen. Jas. D. Morgan, also a cooper, they opened a shop of their own on the site of the present county jail. In connection with this Mr. Wells also carried on the provision and packing business, continuing the two branches for nine years. At the expiration of that time he embarked in pork and beef packing on a large scale, and has been successfully engaged in that business up to within a year.

One of the wealthiest of our citizens, Mr. Wells is also one of our most enterprising and public spirited men. He has served the city efficiently as alderman of the Second Ward, is at present Director of the First

National Bank, of the Quincy, Alton & St. Louis R. R., of the Republic Insurance Co. of Chicago, and President of its local Board, and has been prominent for his untiring energy in behalf of the many railroad projects originated the past few years for the advancement of Quincy.

Few men have done more for Quincy than Edward Wells, and she boasts no more valuable citizen.

EDUCATIONAL.

The citizens of Quincy, with commendable foresight, early turned their attention to providing educational institutions for their children, and at the same time, by establishing public schools secured the benefits of an education to those without parents, or whose parents were unable to bear the expense. While most of the colleges and academies that have been founded here have prospered and become self-sustaining, and while we feel an interest in their success, still the greatest pride our citizens feel is in the noble system of public schools, which through years of struggling and experimenting, have been brought to a high degree of perfection. These schools, which are supported by the taxation of property, are managed by a Board chosen annually by the City Council, and we are thus guaranteed that they will be placed at all times under the control of competent persons.

PUBLIC SCHOOLS.

The Board of Education is composed as follows:— P. A. Goodwin, President, Thos. W. Macfall, Clerk, J. W. Brown, Superintendent of Schools, E. H. Turner, H. H. Mertens, A. J. Lubbe and C. R. Richardson.

The HIGH SCHOOL is situated on Eighth street. A. W. Starkey is principal, Miss M. E. Osborn first and Miss M. R. Kenney second assistant. Total number of pupils enrolled, 75.

The GRAMMAR SCHOOL is in the same building. Miss M. P. Oven and Mrs. M. W. Starkey, teachers. Total number of pupils enrolled, 106.

WASHINGTON SCHOOL is situated on the corner of Sixth and Cherry streets. Teachers—Miss Kate Anderson, Miss Helen C. Turner, Miss Emma Haines, and Miss Amanda Sylvester. Number of pupils enrolled, 202.

JEFFERSON SCHOOL is situated in Jefferson Square. Teachers—Miss Hannah Mahoney, Miss M. S. Kendall, Miss Emma Jones, and Miss Clara H. Keenan. Number of pupils enrolled, 247.

FRANKLIN SCHOOL is situated on Fifth, between York and Kentucky. Teachers—Miss E. F. Kendall, Miss M. A. Crockett, Miss M. E. Welsh, and Mrs. R. J. Day. Number of pupils enrolled, 246.

IRVING SCHOOL is situated on Payson Avenue, between Eighth and Ninth streets. Teachers—Miss Julia W. Burns, Miss Susie Dunn, Miss A. S. Street, and Miss M. A. W. Carpenter. Number of pupils enrolled, 230.

BERRIAN SCHOOL—Corner of Eighth and Van Buren streets. Teachers—Miss Ada R. Lafever, Miss Ella Smith, and Miss Kate Shannahan. Numbers of pupils enrolled, 150.

WEBSTER SCHOOL—Corner of Twelfth and Maine streets. Teachers—Miss E. M. Bryson, Miss Lizzie

Welch, Miss M. E. Randall, Miss Laura Drain, and Miss Mary Allen. Number of pupils enrolled, 318.

MADISON SCHOOL is in East Quincy. Teachers—Miss M. A. McKinnie, and Miss Monia McKinnie. Number of pupils enrolled, 73.

COLORED SCHOOL, No. 1—Oak, between Ninth and Tenth streets. Teacher—Miss M. F. Martin. Number of pupils enrolled, 46.

COLORED SCHOOL, No. 2—Tenth, between Spring and Oak streets. Teacher—Miss W. H. Morgan. Number of pupils enrolled, 75.

Total number of schools, 10; total number of teachers, 31; total amount salaries paid officers and teachers, $17,500; incidental expenses, $4,500. Total number of children enrolled in all the schools, white 1,647, colored 121; total white and colored, 1,768. Average cost to city of each pupil attending public schools, $12.44½.

In addition to the public schools, the following colleges, academies, and schools are well supported and numerously attended:

Quincy College, Spring street, between Third and Fourth streets.

St. Francis College, corner Vine and Eighteenth sts.

Quincy Female Seminary, Eighth, between Maine and Hampshire streets.

Institute of the Infant Jesus, Eighth and Vermont streets.

German Independent School, Eleventh and Jersey streets.

SELECT SCHOOLS.

M. C. Abbe, R. A. Bower, H. A. Farwell, I. Fogg, H. C. Terrell, T. Walker.

SCHOOLS CONNECTED WITH CHURCHES.

Evangelical Zion's Church, each of the German Evangelical, German Evangelical Lutheran, Hebrew, and Roman Catholic Churches.

The public schools, as we have said, have been brought to a high state of perfection, and offer every advantage to those seeking an education. A thorough English education is afforded under the present admirable system of management, and the German language is also taught.

In our colleges not only the English in all its branches is taught, but every opportunity is offered to obtain a thorough knowledge of the classics.

The educational advantages of Quincy are well worthy the attention of those seeking homes in the west, and no city of its size will be found better provided in this respect.

WM. MORRIS, ESQ.,

OR "MEN OF MARK" IN QUINCY.

The subject of this sketch since his residence in Quincy has contributed largely by his enterprise to advance the manufacturing interests of the city.

The question of obtaining coal in abundance and at reasonable rates was one that long agitated our citizens—and Mr. Morris on locating here, began operating the mines at Colchester, and soon developed them to an extent that enabled him to supply us at prices below even Chicago, with all her railroad and water facilities.

A native of New York, Mr. Morris passed the period of his life until he was twenty-three in various cities of the Empire State. In 1840 he proceeded south, and after making an extended tour of the Southern States, located in Mobile, engaging in the wholesale grocery business. Here he remained until 1857, when he came to Quincy, and at once embarked in the coal business, as one of the Quincy Coal Co.

Since engaging in this enterprise he has directed and managed its affairs including its mines at Colchester and yards in this city, with ability and success, making its operations both profitable to the company and satisfactory to the public.

A liberal and estimable gentleman, Mr. Morris ranks as one of the solid men of Quincy.

CHAS. W. KEYES, LEADING MERCHANT.

OR, "MEN OF MARK" IN QUINCY.

Many of the young men of Quincy have within the past few years embarked in business, and taken front rank as active and enterprising merchants.

Of these, Charles W. Keyes, of the leading drug house of Montgomery & Co., is an instance. A native of Quincy, his father being one of the first settlers here, after graduating at Williams College, Mass., in 1864, he made an extended tour through Europe, and then returning to Quincy, embarked in the wholesale drug business, as one of the firm of Montgomery & Co. In business he has been eminently successful, the firm with which he is connected, ranking any in its line in the city. Prudent, but eminently enterprising, and thoroughly devoted to business, Mr. Keyes has a career of uninterrupted prosperity before him.

RELIGIOUS.

There are in Quincy twenty-five churches or places of worship, which speaks well for the moral character of her people. Many of these are imposing and costly edifices, that well deserve an extended notice here, but for want of space we are obliged to forego the pleasure. The various denominations are represented as follows:

BAPTIST—First Baptist Church, First Colored Baptist Church, and Vermont Street Baptist Church.

CHRISTIAN—Church of Christ.

CONGREGATIONAL—1st Union Congregational Church, German Evangelical Zion's Church.

EPISCOPAL—St. John's Church.

GERMAN EVANGELICAL—Salem's Church, St. Jacobi Church.

GERMAN EVANGELICAL LUTHERAN—St. John's Church, St. Peter's Church.

HEBREW—German Reformed Congregation—B' nai Sholoum, K. K. Bnai Abrohom.

METHODIST EPISCOPAL—African M. E. Church, Fifth Street M. E. Church, German M. E. Church, Vermont Street M. E. Church.

PRESBYTERIAN—First Presbyterian Church, Westminster Church.

ROMAN CATHOLIC—St. Aloysius Chapel, St. Boniface Church, St. Francis Church, St. Mary's Church, St. Peter's Church.

UNITARIAN—Second Congregational Society.

H. S. OSBORN, LEADING MANUFACTURER,

OR "MEN OF MARK" IN QUINCY.

We come now to one who has been eminently successful in one of the most important branches of our manufactures, and who has also wielded a large influence in municipal affairs.

H. S. Osborn, senior member of the firm of W. H. Osborn & Co., is a native of England, where he was born June 6th, 1814. Passing his youth in the city of London, where he was born, he there received his education, and when about twenty years of age, emigrated to the United States. He first located in New York city, where he remained two years, at the expiration of which time he removed to Circleville, Ohio, and engaged in the milling business. At the end of three years, he changed his location to Waverly, Ohio, where he again embarked in the milling enterprise. For nine years he continued at Waverly, after which he came to Quincy, arriving here in August, 1846. Purchasing an interest in the old "Eagle Mills" that stood at the corner of Broadway and Front streets, he continued to operate it as one of the firm of Wheeler, Osborn & Co., until it was destroyed by fire. The firm at once proceeded to replace the building destroyed, and in 1852 completed a splendid new edifice, and furnished it with all the equipments and machinery for a first-class flouring mill. This was subsequently sold to the C. B. & Q. R. R. Co., and removed to supply the demand for more yard room. It was upon the sale of this building that the present colossal structure known as the "Eagle Mills" was erected. It was completed in 1867, and is in every respect one of the finest establishments of its kind in the Union. Its equipments are of the most modern style, its machinery of the most approved pattern, and its improvements of the most convenient order.

It is now operated and managed by the firm of W. H. Osborn & Co., of which, as we have said, Mr. Osborn is senior partner, and is one of the most successful institutions of our city.

In addition to being one of the most successful of our citizens, Mr. Osborn is also one of the most valuable. Several times elected to the City Council, his services in that body were marked and beneficial to the city. He has also been active in every public enterprise, and his contributions to the charitable institutions of Quincy have been on a scale of liberality equaled by but few.

A thorough business man, a generous and enterprising citizen, none have contributed more to improve and advance Quincy than H. S. Osborn.

S. J. LESEM, LEADING MERCHANT,

OR, "MEN OF MARK" IN QUINCY.

As the head of the great dry goods house of S. J. Lesem, Bro. & Co., the subject of this sketch has won a reputation for business sagacity and ability that places him in the front rank of the leading merchants of the country.

S. J. Lesem is a native of Bavaria, where he received his business education, and where he remained until the age of 21. He then concluded to come to the United States, and in 1850 he arrived in St. Louis. Remaining there but a few days, he proceeded to Saint Charles county, Mo., where he engaged on a farm, but continued at it only three months. He then commenced peddling, carrying his own pack until he had accumulated sufficient means to buy a horse and wagon. After two years' experience in peddling, Mr. Lesem established himself in the mercantile business in Warrington, Mo., with two partners. At the end of one year he removed to Glasgow in the same state, and obtained employment as clerk in a dry goods house. From there he proceeded to LaFayette county, and went into business with an uncle, with whom he remained 18 months, when he sold out, and came to Quincy. Here, in 1855, in connection with his uncle, S. Lesem, now deceased, he opened a dry goods house. In 1856, he purchased the interest of S. Lesem in the business and associating with his brother Isaac Lesem, conducted the same until 1865, when, associating with them Gustav Levy, they opened the first exclusive wholesale dry goods house ever established in Quincy.

Since then this house has done an immense trade, and its commodious salesrooms are constantly alive with business.

Managed by thorough business men, who have been drilled in the school of experience, its business is daily increasing, and already the house of S. J. Lesem, Bro. & Co. ranks second to few in the west in the quantity and quality of stock carried, and the amount of annual sales.

JOHN W. BROWN, SUP'T OF PUBLIC SCHOOLS,

OR, "MEN OF MARK" IN QUINCY.

None have been more active in the cause of education in Quincy, than the subject of this sketch. John W. Brown is a native of Ohio, being born in Warren county in that state in 1832. His early life was spent upon a farm, where, although required to do hard work, he was afforded the advantages of both a common school and academic education. In 1851 he began teaching school, and for three years, while following this vocation, also devoted himself to perfecting his own studies. In 1855 he came to Quincy, and opened a jewelry store. He is still engaged in this business, as the head of one of the largest establishments in our city.

Mr. Brown early manifested an interest in the educational progress of Quincy, and assisted in the organization of the Board of Education, of which he was the first clerk. Subsequently in 1863 he was again elected to the Board, and in 1865 was made Superintendent of Public Schools by the city council. The past year he was again called to this responsible position, which he still holds, administering its arduous duties with ability and satisfaction. In addition to his services in the cause of education, Mr. Brown has also worked zealously in organizing and conducting Sunday Schools, and is the present Secretary of the Adams County Sunday School Convention. Earnest and persevering, he seldom fails in what he undertakes, and hence he has been able to conduct successfully his extensive jewelry business, while devoting so large a share of his time to the public good.

FIRE DEPARTMENT.

Thirty years ago the citizens of the then modest City of Quincy, commenced the foundation of what has since grown to be one of the strongest and most efficient volunteer fire departments in the Union. At that time most of the "solid men" of Quincy mustered in No. 1 Engine Company, and followed "the machine" when duty called. As a matter of interest, we reproduce a list of the members of this company, when it organized in 1839. Many of them have since passed to that bourne whence no traveler returns, but others will be recognized as active and leading citizens of Quincy to-day.— The following is the roster.

Thomas Jasper,
Amos Green,
Thomas Redmond,
James D. Morgan,
Lorenzo Bull, jr.,
Edward Wells,
Frederick W. Jansen,
Wm. H. Gage,
Samuel Holmes,
I. O. Woodruff,
Hiram Rogers,
F. G. Johnston,
Damon Hauser,
Nathaniel Summers,
James McDade,
Timothy Rogers,
Thomas C. Benneson,
J. A. King
John B. Young,
Wm. H. Tandy,
Joel Thorn,
Charles W. Manson,
Wm. F. Karnes,
Henry Burrell,
J. H. Ralston,
T. C. King,
Louis Cosson,
J. H. Luce,
Adam Schmitt
William Coyne,
Charles McDonald,
Geo. W. Chapman,
John Crockett,
Michael Mast,
E. M. Davis,
L. B. Allen,
J. H. Holton,
Jacob Gruell,
Stedman Nash,
Enoch Conyers,
Wm. G. Flood,
John H. Kreinhop,
Jacob A. Funk,
Charles Albright,
Charles A. Nourse,
Harrison Dills,
T. W. Goodwyn,
C. Vierheller,
John H. Cottle,
J. O. Bernard,
John Paine,
Samuel Winters.

The organization thus started, has now grown to several hundred members, with steam and hand engines of the most approved make, equipped in the most thorough manner, and managed by a Board of Fire Engineers under a most admirable system.

The following is the roster of the department at present:

Henry Meisser, Chief Engineer, J. H. Ayers, First Assistant, Wm. H. Shinn, Second Assistant.

BOARD OF FIRE ENGINEERS—Mayor Berrian, *ex-officio* President; John Tillson, Philip Steinbach, Henry Meisser, William H. Shinn; John H. Ayers Sec'y.

COMPANIES.

QUINCY, No. 1—Steamer James M. Pitman. Tom J. Heirs, Pres., Wm. M. Avise, Vice Pres., E. Eaton, Sec'y, D. G. Williams, Treas.

John Metzger, foreman, T. Dyke, assistant foreman, John W. Schulte, foreman of hose, R. H. Benneson engineer.

WATER WITCH No. 2—Steamer James D. Morgan, and hand engine. Frank Scheiner, foreman, Henry Urmstead assistant foreman, M. McDonnell, sec'y, L. Bull, treas.

LIBERTY No. 3—Hand Engine. Henry Lageman, foreman, Bernard Kathman, sec'y.

NEPTUNE No. 4—Steamer John Wood, and hand engine. John A. Steinbach, foreman, T. S. Clark, assistant foreman, Frank Smith, sec'y, J. Fisher, treas.

Phoenix No. 5—Hand Engine. Henry Steinkamp, foreman, J. L. Pfau, jr., sec'y.

Rough and Ready No. 6—Hand Engine. John Wavering, foreman, Wm. Helmbold, sec'y.

Pioneer Hook and Ladder Co. No. 1—Henry Gail, foreman, Henry Rothgeb, sec'y.

The steamers, hand engines, hose, equipments, and engine houses at present under control of the Board are valued at $57,595.

No city of Quincy's size in the Union is better provided in this respect than is our own, and all that is required to make our security against fire perfect, is the promised water works, which will undoubtedly be built within two years.

Under the present system, public cisterns for the use of the department are built in various portions of the city, and are kept constantly full of water, to be used in case of fire.

The past twelve months we have but fourteen fires to record, only one of which, the C. B. & Q. Freight Depot, was a serious conflagration. The total loss by fire for the year 1869; was $60,050, mostly covered by insurance.

Hon. B. F. BERRIAN, Mayor of Quincy,

OR "MEN OF MARK" IN QUINCY.

The subject of this sketch has ever since coming to Quincy had a large interest in its welfare and prosperity, and though apparently figuring little in active business circles, has wielded an influence second to none of our leading citizens.

Benjamin F. Berrian is a native of the city of New York, where he was born Oct. 2d, 1831. In 1844 he came to Quincy, and commenced farming, at the same time superintending his brother's interests in real estate in and adjacent to the city. Owning a large amount of property in the city, and having an interest in the management of its affairs, in 1857 he was elected to the common council from the 4th ward, and on the expiration of his term in 1859, was re-elected. Retiring from the council in 1861, he mingled little in politics until 1869, when he was nominated for mayor, and elected by the largest majority but one ever given for that office. This position he now fills, discharging its duties in a manner alike creditable to himself and the city.

A man of warm impulses, and genial and affable manners, Mayor Berrian, long before his election to office, was one of the most popular of our citizens, and to-day has as many political and personal friends as any one in the community.

RAILROADS.

Those who have given little time to investigating the history of our railroads, and who were not immediately connected with them, have but a faint idea of the difficulties with which our citizens contended, in successfully carrying out their early enterprises of this kind. Few of those who now enjoy the advantages of the magnificent system of railroads centering here, know, or think of the trials and struggles of their enterprising originators to bring about this grand consummation.— Those however who were intimately connected with these undertakings; and through whose indomitable perseverance and untiring energy they were successfully carried out, can now point with pride to the thoroughly equipped and admirably managed roads entering Quincy as monuments to their sagacity and foresight. Three great lines of road terminate here at present, affording facilities and connections unsurpassed by any city in the Union. The oldest of these roads is the

CHICAGO, BURLINGTON & QUINCY,

Which was completed and put in running order in February, 1856. That part of the road between Quincy and Galesburg, was built by the Northern Cross Railroad Company, and was known as the Northern Cross Railroad until 1857. The history of this road would prove of decided interest to many of our readers who are not conversant with its varied fortunes from its origin to the present time. Want of space, however, prevents us detailing at length these events.

Under the internal improvement system, inaugurated by the State in 1837, various lines of railroad were prescribed by the Legislature, among which was the " Northern Cross Railroad, from Quincy, on the Mississippi river, via Columbus and Clayton in Adams county, Mt. Sterling in Brown county, Meredosia and Jacksonville in Morgan county, Springfield in Sangamon county, Decatur in Macon county, Sidney in Champaign county, and Danville in Vermillion county, thence to the State Line, in the direction of Lafayette, Indiana."

Under this system the State commenced the construction of railroads in various sections of the State, but in the course of three or four years broke down, having expended some $8,000,000, and put in operation only sixty miles of road from Meredosia to Springfield, and this constructed in the most inferior manner. This was a part of the original "Northern Cross Railroad," and was managed by the State for several years, when by order of the Legislature it was sold at public auction.

On the 10th day of February, 1849, the Legislature passed an act incorporating the Northern Cross Railroad Company, with James M. Pitman, Samuel Holmes, John Wood, C. A. Warren, Gershom B. Dimock, Hiram Boyle and Isaac N. Morris of Adams county, and James Brockman and James W. Singleton of Brown county, their associates, successors, assigns, &c., with power to construct, maintain and use a railroad from the west bank of the Illinois river, opposite the town of Meredosia, to the Mississippi river at Quincy:

In pursuance of an act passed by the Legislature in October, 1849, Augustus C. French, then Governor, offered for sale that part of the said old Northern Cross Railroad lying between the Illinois and Mississippi rivers—and James W. Singleton, Samuel Holmes, Horace S. Cooley, Calvin A. Warren, James M. Pitman and Isaac N. Morris became the purchasers for $1850, payable in State indebtedness.

On the road thus purchased, there had been upwards of $500,000 expended by the State between Quincy and Clayton.

At a meeting of the proprietors, on the 19th of February, 1850, it was recommended, " to the present owners of the road to subscribe ten thousand dollars of the capital stock of the same, in proportion to their respective interests therein." In pursuance of this recommendation books were opened, and the proprietors subscribed the following shares.

I. N. Morris 15, J. W. Singleton 15, James M. Pitman 15, Calvin A. Warren 10, Samuel Holmes 15, O. C. Skinner 5, N. Bushnell 5, H. S. Cooley 5, Amos Green 4, Bartlett & Sullivan 3, Henry Asbury 2, Newton Flagg 3, E. Moore 3. Making 100 shares equal to $10,000, the number of shares required to enable the company to formally organize. The following Directors and Officers were then elected:—I. N. Morris, Jas. W. Singleton, Jas. M. Pitman, N. Bushnell, and N. Flagg, Directors—I. N. Morris, Pres., Ebenezer Moore, Treas., and Samuel Holmes, Sec'y.

The Company now purchased from the proprietors,

the road and appurtenances purchased from the State, and prepared for active work. Their efforts however, proved abortive, until the winter of 1850-1, when an arrangement was effected between the company and the citizens of Quincy, by which the city subscribed $100,000 stock, payable in bonds. The company was to have $20,000 of this stock as representing their interest, and a new election of Directors and Officers was to be held.

After this subscription a new election was held, and Nehemiah Bushnell, Hiram Rogers, Lorenzo Bull, Jas. M. Pitman and Jas. D. Morgan were chosen Directors. Nehemiah Bushnell was then elected President.

Under this organization the company went vigorously to work, and located and graded the road from Quincy to Clayton, and had contracted for the necessary iron. The road was also located to Mt. Sterling, and the contracts for the work made with responsible parties, when some dissatisfaction having arisen in Brown county, the company were unable to get the bonds previously subscribed by that county. This important circumstance, together with the further important fact that the Sangamon & Morgan Railroad Co. had always been hostile to a connection with our road, satisfied the company that any further effort to reach the Illinois river at that time was useless.

The object had up to that time been to construct a road from Quincy to Meredosia, but they were now compelled reluctantly to suspend operations in that direction.

It was at this time that the company, resolved upon having a railroad outlet for Quincy, turned its attention northward, and sought other connections. The company previously, in 1851, had procured an act of the Legislature, authorizing them to build a lateral road, branching off from the main line in Adams county in the direction of Chicago, and when they found it impossible to reach the Illinois river they entered into a contract with the Central Military Tract Railroad Co., then organized to build a road north from Galesburg, in which for the purpose of better securing the construction of both roads, it was mutually agreed that neither would contract with any parties for building its road who would not at the same time agree to build the other, so as to secure to both roads a through line from Quincy to Chicago. Prior to this parties interested in the Michigan Central Railroad had acquired control of the Aurora Branch Railroad, extending from Chicago to Mendota, and were desirous of reaching the Mississippi river. In November, 1852, therefore, Nehemiah Bushnell, President of the Northern Cross Railroad Company, proceeded to Detroit, with a view if possible of interesting Messrs. J. W. Brooks and Jas. F. Joy, who represented the parties controlling the Aurora Branch Road, in the immediate construction of our Northern Branch. The negotiations then commenced, led in June, 1853, to a final arrangement for building the entire line from Quincy to Chicago.

The city of Quincy made a further subscription of $100,000, and its citizens also subscribed $100,000.— Other parties along the line now subscribed to the enterprise, and it was pushed forward vigorously, but not without delay and difficulties. In the latter part of January, 1856, the entire road from Quincy to Galesburg was completed at a cost of $3,600,000, and on the first day of February, following, the first through train passed over the road. The road north from Galesburg to Chicago had been completed in the meantime, and thus we had an unbroken line from Quincy to Chicago.— From the time the company was re-organized in 1851, during the whole period of the construction from Quincy to Galesburg, and up to the consolidation as the Chicago, Burlington & Quincy Railroad, in 1861, Nehemiah Bushnell continued President of the Company, with Lorenzo Bull, Jas. D. Morgan, Hiram Rogers, John Wood, and James M. Pitman, Directors.

The road thus built, after so many trials, and under so many difficulties, has now become an integral portion of a long line of consolidated roads, second in importance to none in the west, extending from Quincy to Chicago, and branching from Galesburg to Burlington and Peoria, and through Lewiston and Rushville, embracing in its operations upwards of five hundred miles of first-class roads, perhaps the best equipped, best managed, and most successful business railroad in the whole country. The effect of the completion of this road upon Quincy may well be imagined. Business started anew, and grew to magnificent proportions, our population was augmented by thrifty mechanics and laborers from the east, new branches of manufacture and business were established, and in a short time Quincy merged into an active metropolitan city. Not only were we thus indirectly benefitted, but the road itself established here shops which have since employed hundreds of men, built freight houses where a large number of laborers are constantly engaged; and in various ways contributed to augment the population, and increase the wealth of our city. The next road constructed in which Quincy had a deep interest, and which was a Quincy enterprise, was the road from Quincy to Meredosia, now a part of the

TOLEDO, WABASH & WESTERN RAILWAY.

This road was built under an act of the Legislature of Illinois, incorporating the Quincy and Toledo Railroad, and the route of the road was the one orignally attempted by the Northern Cross Railroad Company, but which was abandoned in consequence of opposition and difficulties met with. Subsequently, Hon. Jas. W. Singleton obtained a charter, and proceeded to construct the road from Camp Point in Adams County, to the Illinois river at Meredosia. In this enterprise, as in the one above quoted, General Singleton met with obstacles that seemed to threaten the success of the project, but with that determination proverbial in him, he fought the road through, and not only completed and set it in operation, but also constructed a bridge for its use over the Illinois.

Building a railroad then and now were vastly different undertakings. Then there was none of that enthusiasm for them that prevails now, and those who had not experimented with them, nor knew the benefits to be derived from their construction, were disposed to stand aloof and withhold their aid and encouragement. Against all obstacles however that presented themselves Gen. Singleton, as we have said, contended, until he constructed a road from Camp Point to the Illinois river. At the Illinois river it connected with what was called the Great Western Railroad, and thus on to Toledo and the seaboard. From Camp Point to Quincy its trains used the track of the C. B. & Q. R. R., and thus it gave us another route from Quincy to the east. The advantages thus secured cannot be over-estimated. Competition in through freight to and from the east followed, and our city was soon placed, as regards railroads and business facilities, on a par with St. Louis, and other western points. After various changes and consolidations, this road finally merged into the Toledo, Wabash & Western Railway, which now forms an unbroken line from Quincy to the east. Like the C. B. & Q., this road is managed by experienced and thorough railroad men, and is equipped and stocked in a style unsurpassed by any road in the Union. The last of our roads built was the Quincy & Palmyra, which has since merged into the

HANNIBAL & ST. JOSEPH RAIL ROAD.

This road is virtually the Quincy & St. Joseph, as most of its freight and business passes over the Quincy Railroad Bridge at this point. That part of the road known as the Quincy & Palmyra, and which was built by our citizens, although only twelve miles long, was a very important item to our city. The Hannibal & St. Joseph Railroad, which runs entirely across the State of Missouri had been built, and made its eastern terminus at Hannibal. It penetrated a country naturally tributary to Quincy, and was thus pouring into Hannibal the wealth and produce of this region. To checkmate this it required only twelve miles of railroad from Quincy to Palmyra, to connect us with the Hannibal & St. Joseph Railroad, and thus afford our merchants and business men speedy communication with the citizens along its line.

Our prominent citizens realizing the situation at once put their shoulders to the wheel, and the Quincy & Palmyra Railroad Company was promptly organized, with Col. Samuel Holmes as its President. Unfortunately, it began operations in 1856, and about the time it commenced work in earnest the crisis of 1857 lowered upon the country, stagnating business, and retarding enterprises of every kind. Notwithstanding this the road was completed in 1859, and operated as an independent road for many years. In 1866 it was purchased by the Hannibal & St. Joseph Railroad, and thus we have an unbroken line from Quincy to St. Joseph, Mo., and thence on to the Pacific coast.

This road is now one of the best constructed and safest roads in the country, and its management comprises some of the most experienced and skillful railroad men in the Union.

REMARKS.

It is difficult to estimate the benefits derived from these roads by our city. Each gives employment to a large number of men, and annually spends large sums of money. Their freight houses, machine shops, and offices are constantly alive with the din and bustle of business, and are a marked acquisition to our city. The amount of territory made tributary to Quincy by these iron ties, and the wealth and products annually brought here, are considerations of importance that must be realized by every thinking citizen, and we should therefore hail with delight every move to increase our facilities in this respect, and extend our present admirable system.

HORSE RAILWAY.

Quincy is decidedly an enterprising city, and is always prompt to advantage herself of such modern improvements as are calculated to advance her interests, or benefit her citizens. It was not strange, therefore, that she should follow in the wake of other metropolitan cities, and secure a horse railway. This enterprise was completed in the fall of 1867, and has been in operation since. Although only a mile and a half long, it is well patronized, and cars run at intervals of half an hour during the day, and until late at night. It is contemplated to extend it at an early day.

U. S. PENFIELD, CASHIER 1ST NATIONAL BANK.

OR, "MEN OF MARK" IN QUINCY.

Few men have been more intimately identified with the progress and development of Quincy, than U. S. Penfield, Cashier First National Bank.

A native of New York, as early as 1838 he cast his fortunes with our city, locating here and engaging in the mercantile business. Subsequently he engaged in the milling business, and with John B. Brown, now deceased, erected the Star Mills, that stood near the corner of Front and Spring streets, and were removed to give way to the C. B. & Q. R. R. depot and yards. Upon the retirement of Mr. Clark, first cashier of the Quincy Savings Bank, now the First National, Mr. Penfield was called to that responsible position, which he has filled for eleven years. His services in this position are known to the entire business community of Quincy, and the best evidence of their appreciation by the bank is to be found in his repeated election by its Directors, and the liberal salary paid him by the institution.

Possessed of rare business qualifications, and devoted to the duties of his position, Mr. Penfield has as Cashier of the First National Bank, made a reputation as a skilled and thorough financier, and also won the confidence and esteem of every citizen of Quincy.

FAVORITE ROUTE EAST

CHICAGO,
BURLINGTON AND QUINCY
RAILROAD LINE.

Passengers going East by this route have the advantage of

3 Through Express Trains Daily

FROM KANSAS CITY, ST. JOSEPH, AND QUINCY

Making close and sure connections at Chicago with the Four Great Through Lines to the East.

ONLY ONE CHANGE OF CARS

From Kansas City or Quincy to

NIAGARA FALLS, CLEVELAND, BUFFALO, PITTSBURG

Rochester, Syracuse, Albany, Columbus,

HARRISBURG, PHIL'A, NEW YORK,

And other principal points East.

CHICAGO,
BURLINGTON AND QUINCY
RAILROAD LINE.

THE ONLY ROAD FROM QUINCY

Giving passengers a choice of THREE DIFFERENT ROUTES to NEW YORK, with but one change of cars.

Elegant Twelve-Wheeled Coaches and Sleeping Cars
Accompany all Express Trains.

THE ONLY ROUTE RUNNING
PULLMAN'S MAGNIFICENT SLEEPING COACHES!
From Quincy on All Night Trains.

Through Tickets Sold at all Principal Offices
At as low Rates as by any other Route.

BAGGAGE CHECKED THROUGH AND HANDLED FREE.

☞ Passengers going East should be particular to ASK FOR TICKETS VIA CHICAGO.

ROBERT HARRIS,	E. A. PARKER,
Gen'l Sup't, Chicago.	Gen. West. Pass. Agt., Chicago.

PROJECTED RAILROADS.

During the past year our citizens have taken steps to vastly strengthen and extend the railroad system of which Quincy is the center. At least three new roads have been projected, and are now placed upon a basis that guarantees their speedy completion. These roads are the Quincy, Missouri & Pacific, the Quincy & Carthage, and the Quincy, Alton & St. Louis. In addition to these may also be mentioned the Mississippi & Missouri River Air Line Railroad, whose organization is of an older date, and upon which considerable work has already been done. This also has its eastern terminus in this city. The

QUINCY, MISSOURI & PACIFIC R. R.

which may be emphatically called a Quincy institution, having first had life and stability infused into it by the genius and enterprise of our citizens, has progressed in public favor with wondrous rapidity ever since the formal organization of the company at Kirksville, in June last, and already the preliminary survey has been made, and the route is now being located. The length of the proposed line is estimated at 230 miles, and under the laws of Missouri relating to railroads, the necessary one thousand dollars per mile was subscribed, and five per cent. paid in at the date of organization. The route of the road is from West Quincy, thence north-west through the counties of Marion, Lewis, Knox via Edina, Adair via Kirksville, Sullivan, Grundy, Harrison, Gentry, Nodaway and Atchison, in the State of Missouri, to a point on the east bank of the Missouri river, opposite the city of Brownville, Nebraska. On the preliminary survey, recently completed, a very favorable line was found from river to river, with a maximum grade of sixty-six feet to the mile, and with easy curvatures throughout.

Municipal subscriptions to the amount of $1,200,000 have already been voted to this road, and arrangements made for taking the vote of other counties and townships for additional subscriptions to the amount of $1,100,000.

The Directors of this Company are Ex-Gov. Wood, C. A. Savage, Thomas Redmond, Thomas Jasper, C. H. Bull, T. R. Selmes, C. M. Pomroy, Geo. Adams, John Winterbottom, W. C. Hillis, J. M. DeFrance, M. G. Roseberry, and J. S. Church. The officers are Chas. A. Savage, Pres., Geo. S. King, Sec'y., C. H. Bull, Treas., and John H. Schermerhorn, Chief Engineer.

Under the management and direction of citizens of such acknowledged energy and enterprise, it may be safely anticipated that the 1st of January, 1871 will find this road far on its way to completion, when another triumph in the consummation of Quincy's greatness will have been achieved.

Not less progressive has been the

QUINCY & CARTHAGE R. R.,

Since the organization of that Company. Its Directors and Officers at once set to work with commendable energy, and have the completion of their road at an early date guaranteed beyond peradventure. This Company also was the creation of the year 1870, and organized with the following Directors:—O. C. Skinner, Thomas Jasper, Samuel R. Chittenden, Hiram G. Ferris and David A. Patterson.

Hon. O. C. Skinner was chosen President, James M. Bishop, Sec'y., and Hiram G. Ferris, Treasurer.

The route of this road is almost due north from Quincy, passing through Mendon and Keene townships in Adams county, thence on through St. Albans, Bear Creek and Prairie townships in Hancock county, to Carthage, where connections with other roads are contemplated that will open up to Quincy a vast section of rich territory, besides affording her another railroad outlet to the lakes and seaboard.

Some $300,000 in subscriptions has been voted to this road, and we learn that work will be commenced at once, grading and tieing the same, the survey being nearly completed.

This will form an important item in our railroad system, and will pour into our city untold wealth and commerce that has heretofore been isolated from the market.

Another important road, and one that our business interests have long demanded, is the

QUINCY, ALTON & ST. LOUIS R. R.

A company to construct this railroad was organized September 10th, 1869, with the following Directors:— Jas. W. Singleton, R. S. Benneson, A. J. F. Prevost, Wm. Bowles, C. H. Curtis, Edward Wells, Eli Seehorn, Perry Alexander, and C. L. Higbee. The officers are Jas. W. Singleton, Pres., Thomas T. Woodruff, Sec'y and Treasurer.

All of the gentlemen identified with this road are men of untiring energy and enterprise, to several of whom our city is already indebted for many enterprises of a public character that have been potent in advancing her in wealth or commercial prestige. Although the last of the companies organized the past year, it has prepared for earnest work, and a corps of engineers are in the field engaged in the preliminary survey.

The route of this road will propably be almost due south, via Payson, Barry, and on to Alton and St. Louis. $200,000 has now been voted to the road by Adams county, while a considerable additional sum will undoubtedly be voted by townships along the proposed route after the survey has been made. Several of the richest counties in the State will be penetrated by this road, and it will result in vast advantage to the trade and commerce of Quincy. A direct connection will also be formed with St. Louis, which cannot fail to prove mutually beneficial.

MISSISSIPPI & MISSOURI RIVER AIR-LINE R. R.

Although of older date than any of the above, properly comes within this article, it being now in process of construction. It also has its eastern teminus at Quincy, from which it runs north to LaGrange and Canton, and thence west to Memphis, &c. Considerable aid has been voted this road and the management are pushing it forward with vigor and industry. A large force of hands are now at work between Quincy and LaGrange, and it is anticipated that the road between Quincy and Canton will be ready for the iron the coming spring.

With these roads completed, what an era of prosperity must dawn upon Quincy, and what strides she will make in the race for metropolitan superiority. Her trade must rapidly increase, her population largely augment, her manufactures extend in every department until her commercial wealth and power declare her master of the upper Mississippi.

WENDELIN WEBER, CONTRACTOR,

OR "MEN OF MARK" IN QUINCY.

The subject of this sketch ranks with the most enterprising of our citizens, and has contributed his full share to the prosperity of Quincy.

Wendelin Weber was born in Hesse Darmstadt, Germany, where he received his education, and also learned the trade of a stone cutter. In 1838 he emigrated to the United States, and the same year located in Quincy. Arriving here without a dollar he at once obtained work at his trade, and by his energy and industry soon acquired sufficient means to establish himself in business as a contractor. At this he has been very successful, and in addition to erecting many buildings for others, and contracting extensively in the city, and on various railroads, Mr. Weber has also built several fine structures on his own account, that add materially to the wealth and beauty of Quincy.

In 1867 Mr. Weber was elected a member of the City Council, and on the expiration of his term in 1869, was re-elected to the same position. As a member of this body he has been active and energetic, and has efficiently served the city. Generous and public spirited, no citizen of Quincy has been more earnest in advancing her interests than Wendelin Weber.

PASSENGERS GOING WEST

— TO —

Missouri, Kansas, Nebraska, Colorado, New Mexico, Utah, Idaho, Nevada, California,

Should buy tickets via the short route

HANNIBAL & ST. JOSEPH
RAILROAD LINE.

THREE
DAILY EXPRESS TRAINS

From Quincy or Macon to St. Joseph,

ALSO DIRECT TO

KANSAS CITY!

Without Change of Cars!

Connections are close and direct for

Atchison, Weston,

— AND —

LEAVENWORTH.

Other Connections are made

At St. Joseph with St. Joseph & Council Bluffs R. R.

AT OMAHA WITH

NEBRASKA UNION PACIFIC R. R. FOR FORT KEARNEY, CHEYENNE, UINTAH, PROMONTORY, SACRAMENTO, SAN FRANCISCO, &c.,

And at Cheyenne with Daily Overland Stages for Denver, Central City, Salt Lake, and the Mining Regions.

At Kansas City with Kansas Pacific Railway for

LAWRENCE, OTTAWA, TOPEKA, FORT RILEY, JUNCTION CITY, FORT HAYS, SHERIDAN,

Daily Overland Coaches via Smoky Hill Route leave the Western Terminus Kansas Pacific Railway for

Denver, Central City, Santa Fe,

And all Points in the Mining Regions.

At Kansas City with Mo. River, Ft. Scott & Gulf R. R. for

FT. SCOTT, CHEROKEE NEUTRAL LANDS, FT. GIBSON, **GALVESTON**, &c.

Through Tickets for Sale at all Ticket Offices!

P. B. GROAT, General Ticket Agt.

GEORGE H. NETTLETON, General Sup't.

F. D. SCHERMERHORN, GEN. AGT. T. W. & W. R. W.,

OR, "MEN OF MARK" IN QUINCY.

None of the young men of Quincy who have figured in business circles possess in a greater degree the confidence and esteem of our citizens than Frank D. Schermerhorn, General Agent Toledo, Wabash & Western Railway at this point.

A native of New York, he came to Quincy in 1852, and for a time engaged with his brother, John H. Schermerhorn, present Chief Engineer of the Q. M. & P. R. R., in the survey of the Northern Cross, now the C. B. & Q. R. R. Upon the completion of this road he served in the capacity of ticket agent at this point for a short time, which position he yielded to accept that of bookkeeper in the Quincy Savings Bank. This position he retained for a number of years, rendering eminent satisfaction to his employers, and resigned to embark in the commission business. Soon after his rare worth and business qualifications received a marked recognition at the hands of the Merchants' Despatch Company, by which he was called to the responsible position of Superintendent of its western division, with headquarters at Indianapolis. This position he resigned to accept the General Agency of the T. W. & W. R. W. at

Quincy, which he now fills, administering its affairs with jealous care for the interests of the company, and with eminent satisfaction to our citizens.

Indefatigable in the discharge of the duties intrusted to him, and ever faithful to the interests of his employers, Mr. Schermerhorn has never found it necessary to seek a position, nor has he ever proved unequal to any in which he has been placed.

RIVER COMMERCE.

Notwithstanding the superior railroad facilities enjoyed by Quincy, her citizens are not unmindful of the vast advantage we possess in having the great Father of Waters flowing before us, and affording us cheap transportation north and south. The facilities offered are annually improving, and for nine months of the year we have three or four steamers passing each way daily. The St. Louis & Keokuk and Northern Line Packet Companies' magnificent steamers are at our wharf daily during the season of navigation; and do a large business in carrying freight and passengers to and from our city.

In addition to these we have also the boats of the Eagle Company, plying regularly between Quincy and Keokuk, and transient boats to points above and below.

The accommodations provided by these steamers, for passengers and shippers, are not excelled by any lines in the Union, and hence the large amount of patronage extended to them. The following are the regular steamers plying to and from our city, and the number of through trips made during the season of 1869.

ST. LOUIS & KEOKUK PACKET CO.
FROM ST. LOUIS TO KEOKUK.

NAME OF STEAMER.	NO. OF TRIPS.
J. H. Johnson	82
Andy Johnson	80
Rob Roy	79
Lucy Bertram	4
Bayard	2

NORTHERN LINE PACKET COMPANY.

FROM ST. LOUIS TO ST. PAUL.

Minnesota	18
Minneapolis	11
Sucker State	20
Hawkeye State	10
Dubuque	17
Canada	9
Davenport	3
Phil Sheridan	19
Tom Jasper	19
Milwaukee	16
City of St. Paul	16
Mollie McPike	18

EAGLE PACKET COMPANY.

FROM QUINCY TO KEOKUK.

Grey Eagle	260
Little Eagle	7

In addition to these there were a number of transient steamers and smaller craft, of which no record is kept. No accurate statement of the receipts and shipments from Quincy by these steamers can be obtained, but the business done by them in a season is enormous.

THE QUINCY FERRY COMPANY

Also keeps two boats in active service here, crossing freight and passengers over the river. Capt. John Taylor is the owner and manager of this line, and has two staunch boats, the Rosa Taylor and Quincy.

JOSEPH D. LEVY, LEADING MERCHANT.

OR, "MEN OF MARK" IN QUINCY.

The subject of this sketch is the head of one of the most extensive jobbing houses in the city.

Joseph D. Levy is a native of Germany, where he was born in 1830. Receiving a business education at Stuttgard, at the age of nineteen he emigrated to the United States, locating at Louisville in 1849. After remaining there four years in the mercantile and importing business, he was called by the death of his father to Germany. Returning almost immediately to Louisville, he resumed the mercantile business, and remained there until 1855, when he removed to Canton, Mo., and there opened a dry goods house. In August, 1869, he came to Quincy, and in connection with S. J. Lesem, Isaac Lesem, Emil Levy, and Gustav Levy, established the firm of J. D. Levy & Co., opening one of the most extensive wholesale clothing houses in the west.

Shrewd, sagacious, and untiring in business, prosperity has attended Mr. Levy in all his enterprises, and this last promises to meet with a success greater than any of his former undertakings.

CAPT. F. S. LEE, ST. LOUIS & KEOKUK PACKET CO.,

OR "MEN OF MARK" IN QUINCY.

As commander of the famous steamer J. H. Johnson, and as representative of the St. Louis & Keokuk Packet Company, whose boats have for twenty-eight years plied to and from our city, Capt. Fi S. Lee is well and favorably known to our business community.

A native of Kentucky, Capt. Lee commenced life in mercantile pursuits, but in 1850 accepted a position as clerk of a steamboat. From 1850 to 1865 he continued on the river, most of the time being in the employ of the St. Louis & Keokuk Packet Co. In the latter year he located at Quincy and opened a livery stable. He remained here but nine months, when he resumed steamboating, commanding a boat in the Memphis & Little Rock trade. In 1867 he was again called into the service of the St. Louis & Keokuk Co., and placed in command of the steamer J. H. Johnson, which position he still retains. In addition to his duties as commander during the season of navigation, Capt. Lee during the winter months has charge of the company's boats at this point, superintending their repairs, &c.

An experienced and faithful officer, a popular and accomplished gentleman, Capt. Lee is esteemed wherever he is known for his rare traits of character, and is recognized by our entire community as a valuable citizen of Quincy.

J. T. BRADFORD, LEADING MANUFACTURER,

OR "MEN OF MARK" IN QUINCY.

The subject of this sketch has in a residence of sixteen years proven a valuable citizen, and a sagacious and successful business man. Josiah T. Bradford is a native of Maine, where he passed the period of his life until he was twenty-eight years of age. Before leaving his native State he engaged in the lumber business, and acquired a thorough knowledge of the same. In 1854 he came to Quincy, and with his brother, J. W. Bradford, embarked in the livery business, and continued at it with marked success until 1864.

Previous to retiring from this business, in connection with Robert W. McCoy and J. W. Bradford, he established the firm of Bradford, McCoy & Co., and opened an extensive lumber yard in this city. About the same time this firm also purchased large tracts of land in the pineries of Wisconsin, and established mills for the manufacture of lumber. At present they manufacture on an extensive scale at these mills, and annually bring to our market large quantities of lumber, lath and shingles. The past year this firm also established a yard and planing mills at West Quincy, opposite this city, from which they supply the western trade. Their business has now grown to magnificent proportions, and in order to more speedily supply the demands made up on them from the west, they are about establishing branch yards at Fort Scott, Kansas, and Brownville, Nebraska. Their sales for 1869 were 7,000,000 feet of lumber, 4,000,000 shingles, and 1,000,000 lath. Composed of men of strict integrity and large business experience, this firm is but in the beginning of its prosperity, and gives promise of largely augmenting its trade in the future.

In addition to his services as a leading business man Mr. Bradford has also at all times evinced commendable public spirit in aiding and encouraging railroads, and other enterprises, and served the city efficiently as member of the Council from 1864 to 1866:

CEMETERIES.

In the location and arrangement of its cemeteries, Quincy displays the same refined taste that has prevailed in all her public and private improvements. To the south, beautiful "Woodland," with its treasure of departed hopes interred, sleeps calmly on the proud hills that overlook the broad Mississippi, and as that grand old river marches with a dirge-like tread to the sea, the murmur of its rippling waves is answered by the rustle of the tall oaks that tower like faithful sentinels in this charmed "City of the Dead."

To the east are the Catholic cemeteries, and to the north, also overlooking the river, is that of the Hebrew societies. In all, the genius and skill of the sculptor and artist have been lavishly employed to commemorate the virtues and adorn the graves of the cherished dead.

Peculiarly beautiful however is Woodland, with its graveled roads, winding paths and tufted mounds.— Musing there, one wonders how nature could have been more faithful in molding a home for those who, having fought life's varied battles, sink into that sleep whose waking is immortality,

HENRY FRANK, LEADING MERCHANT,

OR, "MEN OF MARK" IN QUINCY.

The subject of this sketch has resided only a short time in Quincy, but since locating here has by his thorough integrity, rare business qualifications and marked enterprise, won the confidence and esteem of all our citizens. As a partner in the old and established house of Spiegel, Thoms & Co., extensive furniture manufacturers of Indianapolis, Mr. Frank came to Quincy in 1867, and established a branch house, opening with a magnificent stock in the commodious building that then stood on the present site of the *Evening Journal* office. Scarcely a year had elapsed before a disastrous conflagration swept away this establishment, destroying nearly its entire contents, and entailing a heavy loss upon the firm. Undismayed by this stern visitation, Mr. Frank, as the representative of the firm, at once secured the imposing business edifice now occupied by the firm, promptly filled it with a more extensive and more valuable stock than that previously carried by the house, and proceeded to repair the damage and recover the losses caused by the fire. His career had been marked by such unwavering integrity and commendable enterprise, that in the effort to recuperate the business of his firm, and again establish it as a permanent institution of Quincy, he was seconded by the encouragement of our leading citizens, and it was soon in operation in new quarters upon a more extended scale than ever.

Since then the house of Spiegel, Thoms & Co. has prospered beyond the most sanguine expectations of its founders, and is now one of the leading institutions of Quincy. From the extensive manufactories of the firm in Indianapolis, the house in this city is constantly supplied with the finest and best furniture made in the west, and is thus enabled to offer decided advantages in quality and price to its patrons. Managed by Mr. Frank, who is thoroughly versed in the business, the house has now built up an extensive trade in Western Illinois, North Missouri and Southern Iowa, and is destined to still greater success in the future.

AUSTIN BROOKS, Editor "Quincy Herald,"

OR "MEN OF MARK" IN QUINCY.

We have spoken elsewhere of the "Press" of Quincy and its character and influence, and come now to one who has figured for over a quarter of a century as editor of one of our leading journals.

Austin Brooks was born at Cincinnati, from whence he migrated to Illinois with his parents, when only four years of age. His early years were passed in a printing office, his father having established and published successively the *Illinois State Gazette,* at Jacksonville, and the *Alton Commercial Gazette,* in the city of that name. After years of experience in his father's printing offices, being yet quite young, he was sent to McKendrie College, at Lebanon, Ill., but remained only one year, when he embarked on a New Orleans steamer, with the intention of becoming an engineer. At this he continued only a short time, when, coming to Quincy on a steamboat in 1842, he left the river, and commenced work in the *Herald* office, which was then owned by his uncle, John H. Pettit, who also established the *Herald.* Since then Mr. Brooks has been, with scarce an interruption, connected with the *Herald* as chief editor, and was for many years one of the proprietors of the establishment.

An original and powerful writer, he early attained prominence as a journalist, and has been for years recognized as one of the first political writers of the State. A zealous partisan and unflinching Democrat, his time, talents and money have at all times been at the service of his party, and few men have worked more devotedly in the political arena than Austin Brooks. Although repeatedly declining political honors or emoluments, he has served in the legislature of the State, and as Post Master of Quincy. At present editor of the *Herald*, in which position he has passed more than a score of years, his vigorous and ready pen is a power for good in the community, while his forcible writings are read throughout the west, where he has made his mark as one of the ablest editors of the day.

EXECUTIONS.

For a city of its population the criminal record of Quincy has at all times presented an agreeably brief appearance, and as a rule, we have escaped the grave crimes that usually shock metropolitan communities. The moral character and intelligence of our citizens have guarded Quincy in this respect, and have given her a reputation for peace and quiet enjoyed by but few citizens of 40,000 inhabitants. In a period of thirty-six years, and in fact from its first settlement as a town, only two executions have occurred in our city, and these were in each instance for murders committed in the county.

The first was the execution of Thomas C. Bennett, who was found guilty of the murder of John Williams, in 1834. The murder was a cold blooded affair, and Bennett, who was a desperate character, expiated his crime on the gallows, Monday, December 22d, 1834.—The scene of the execution was about the spot now occupied by Dr. Sturgiss' residence.

From that date until 1861, the gallows was not again called into requisition in Quincy. In the latter year, Attison Cunningham and Nelson Cunningham murdered in cold blood a feeble old man named Harrison, who lived some miles south of Quincy, and was supposed to possess some money. For this great crime Attison

Cunningham swung from a gallows in the rear of the court house, Friday morning, Nov. 29th, 1861.

The hanging of Roe, the bushwhacker, in 1865 by a mob, presents the only instance we believe where our citizens have taken the law into their own hands, and is the only stain upon our character as a law abiding community.

NEHEMIAH BUSHNELL, ESQ.,

OR, "MEN OF MARK" IN QUINCY.

It is hardly necessary to preface this sketch with the assertion of the eminent ability, marked services, and irreproachable character of its subject. His achievements as a prominent and public spirited citizen of Quincy are as household words in the community, while his great qualities of head and heart displayed in social life are not less familiar.

A native of Connecticut, Nehemiah Bushnell received his education in that State, graduating at Yale College in 1835. Entering Harvard Law School, he passed the greater portion of the years 1836-7 in this institution, and then returning home completed his law studies in the office of Samuel Ingham, then one of the most eminent lawyers of New England.

Admitted to the bar in 1837, he immediately came west, locating at Quincy. On the 20th of December, in the same year, he commenced the practice of law with his present partner, Hon. O. H. Browning: and this professional association has since continued without interruption. Shortly after establishing himself here the publication of the *Quincy Whig* was commenced, and Mr. Bushnell, assisted by Andrew Johnson, also an attorney, conducted its editorial department, both volunteering their services. Subsequently these gentlemen surrendered their editorial responsibilities, and Mr. Bushnell has since devoted himself exclusively to his profession.

As a lawyer he promptly took rank as the peer of the most gifted men in the State, and adding to his native powers, untiring energy and industry, soon attracted a large and lucrative practice. This he retains to the present day.

Although zealously devoted to his profession, and indefatigable in the interests of his clients, Mr. Bushnell has engaged largely in public enterprises for the advancement of Quincy. As President of the Northern Cross Railroad for many years, and the Quincy Railroad Bridge Company, he was instrumental in achieving for our city two of the grandest enterprises in its history and progress. An active friend of education and science he has aided materially in their development, while in promoting the religious and moral status of Quincy his efforts have been not less marked. In brief, no one citizen has accomplished more for Quincy, and none more justly or more universally esteemed than Nehemiah Bushnell.

HON. J. W. SINGLETON, PRES. Q. & ST. L. R. R.,

OR, "MEN OF MARK" IN QUINCY.

While many of our citizens have been eminent in law, politics, and commerce, the subject of this sketch is perhaps more widely known than any of them, in consequence of his great achievements as a public spirited citizen, and distinguished character as a man.

Hon. James W. Singleton is a native of Virginia, from whence, after finishing his education, he removed to Indiana, being then only 17 years old. Remaining only one year in the Hoosier State, he came to Illinois, locating in Schuyler county. Here he practiced medicine for a while, and also devoted himself to the study of law. Subsequently he farmed successfully, and while thus engaged, was elected twice to the Legislature, and also to the Constitutional convention of 1818, from Schuyler county. During the Mormon troubles at Nauvoo, he was assigned by the Governor of the State command of the military ordered to that point, and remained there until the troubles were satisfactorily adjusted.

In 1852 he came to Quincy, and at once identified himself with every enterprise promising advantage to our city. Earnestly advocating the necessity of railroads, he was untiring in his efforts to secure them to Quincy, and singly and alone constructed the road from Camp Point to the Illinois River at Meredosia. Only the indomitable energy and determination of the man could have accomplished this great success.

He served one term in the Legislature as representative from Adams county, and through his influence in that body accomplished much for Quincy. His mission to Richmond during the war is known to the whole country. Honestly opposed to the war, and believing it to be all wrong, he declined positions of honor and emolument in the army, and remained quietly at home. An intimate and warm friend of President Lincoln, and believing that there were better means of obtaining peace than through war, at the request of the President he visited Richmond, in the hope of dissuading the Confederates from continuing the fratricidal struggle, with a view to an amicable settlement of the difficulties. From causes beyond his control the mission failed, and after twice visiting the Confederate capital, he returned to Quincy. Here he enjoyed the quiet and luxury of his beautiful suburban residence and farm, "Boscobel," until the fall of 1868, when he was unanimously nominated by the Democracy of the Fourth Congressional District as their candidate for Congress. Notwithstanding his great personal popularity, and the fact that he lead his ticket in almost every township, the political complexion of the district was so strongly Republican, that he met with defeat. Since then he has devoted his time to his farm, but recently has taken hold of another enterprise that promises largely to benefit Quincy. This is the Quincy, Alton & St. Louis Railroad, of which he is President, and which he is getting into shape for speedy construction.

Thus identified with nearly all our public enterprises, and filling many places of honor and trust, few men have been so eminently valuable to Quincy as Hon. James W. Singleton, and none rank him in the admiration and esteem of the citizens of Quincy, and the State of Illinois.

E. H. TURNER, LEADING MANUFACTURER,

OR "MEN OF MARK" IN QUINCY.

In a brief residence in Quincy, the subject of this sketch has displayed a vigor, enterprise and ability in business that have made him a marked man in the community.

Coming to Quincy in 1862, he established the house of Turner, VanHorn & Co., which at once commenced the manufacture of tobacco on an extensive scale.— Since then this has grown to be one of the most important of our manufacturing interests, employing annually several hundred hands, and adding materially to our wealth and population. In addition to operating extensively in tobacco, Mr. Turner engaged in packing pork one season, and as in his regular business made it decidedly profitable.

The owner at present of the largest factory in Quincy, and a man of wealth, Mr. Turner is one of the most liberal and enterprising of our citizens, and is universally esteemed as an energetic and sagacious business man, and an accomplished and thorough gentleman.

CITY GOVERNMENT.

1864.

MAYOR,
THOMAS REDMOND.

ALDERMEN.

First Ward—Matthias Obert.
Second " —Moses Jacobs.
Third   " —Maitland Boon.
           Vacancy of A. C. Marsh, deceased.
  "   " —Michael McVay.
Fourth " —Daniel C. Wood.
Fifth   " —John Smith.
Sixth   " —Henry A. Geise.

1865.

MAYOR.
G. F. WALDHAUS.

ALDERMEN.

First Ward—John Whitbread.
Second " —Maitland Boon.
Third   " —Wm. Schrieber.
Fourth " —Ludwig Schroeder.
Fifth   " —Clemens Kathman.
Sixth   " —John Hutton.

1866.

MAYOR.
M. BOON.

ALDERMEN.
First Ward—J. A. Sylvester.
Second   "   —J. T. Bradford.
Third   "   —C. H. Curtis.
Fourth   "   —Wm. Tansman.
Fifth   "   —Thomas Redmond.
Sixth   "   —C. A. Van Den Boom.

1867.

MAYOR.
JAMES M. PITMAN.

ALDERMEN.
First Ward—F. H. Aldrich.
Second   "   —G. H. Davis.
Third   "   —L. F. Lakey.
Fourth   "   —John Tillson.
Fifth   "   —Wendelin Weber.
Sixth   "   —E. W. B. Newby.

1868.

MAYOR
P. W. LANE.

ALDERMEN.
First Ward—H. S. Osborn.
                    Resigned April 5th, 1869.
Second   "   —Wm. Gray.
Third   "   —Philip Steinbach.
Fourth   "   —F. W. Menke.
Fifth   "   —Thomas Redmond.
Sixth   "   —J. G. Rowland.

1869.

MAYOR.
B. F. BERRIAN.

ALDERMEN.

First Ward—Henry Meisser.
" " —W. S. M. Anderson.
                      To fill vacancy of Osborn, resigned.
Second " —I. H. Miller.
Third " —Albert Beebe.
Fourth " —John Tillson.
Fifth " —Wendelin Weber.
Sixth " —A. E. Wheat.

Hon. THOMAS REDMOND,

OR, "MEN OF MARK" IN QUINCY.

In reviewing the history and experiences of the prominent men of our city, few if any will be found who commenced the struggle of life with brilliant prospects. Most of those who have achieved success here purchased it through years of industry and labor, but nevertheless it came steadily and surely. Such is the history and experience of the subject of this sketch.

Thomas Redmond is a native of Ireland, from whence he emigrated to the United States when only sixteen years of age. Thus early he was thrown upon his own resources, and locating in Vermont he obtained employment at whatever offered. After passing several years in New England, he resolved to seek a home in the west. Visiting St. Louis, he started up the Mississippi, and after a brief sojourn in Burlington, Iowa, and Galena, Illinois, he returned down the river and located in Quincy in 1837. Without capital and among strangers, but young and vigorous, he at once obtained employment here. Industrious and energetic, success attended him, and he soon accumulated capital enough to purchase a few horses, carts, wagons, &c., and in company with the late Samuel Holmes and Wm. Shannahan, obtained a contract for grading on the old Northern Cross Railroad, between Quincy and Clayton. At this business he continued with success for many years, being at different times member of the firms of Holmes, Redmond & Shannahan, Redmond, Donlevy & Co., Redmond, Powers & Smith, and Redmond & Holmes. While thus engaged he invested largely in real estate in and adjoining Quincy, which increased in value with the growth of the city.

In 1848 he was elected to the City Council, and since then has been with the exception of two or three years a member of that body. In 1860, upon the resignation of Mayor Woodruff, he was elected to fill the vacancy almost without opposition. For the three successive terms following, he was also elected to the office of mayor, and resigned in 1864, to accept a seat in the Legislature to which he had been chosen. Now the veteran of the City Council, in which he has served for twenty-one years as alderman and mayor, he is recognized as a valuable servant of the city. Enterprising and liberal, he has been among the foremost of our citizens in advancing the commercial and social status of Quincy. Possessed of large wealth, he has employed it to improve the city in which he accumulated it, and has added a number of handsome structures to the business portion of Quincy.

A man of iron will and stern integrity, he seldom fails to accomplish what he undertakes, and few men have had a more successful career, while none stand higher in the esteem of its citizens.

HON. O. C. SKINNER,

OR "MEN OF MARK" IN QUINCY.

The subject of this sketch is another of the prominent men whose pre-eminent genius and mighty intellect has shone out in that illustrious body—the bar of Quincy.

O. C. Skinner was born in Oneida County, New York, where he remained until the age of fifteen, when he made a trip to the Indian country of Lake Superior, and the north. Subsequently he visited Prairie du Chien, Chicago and Milwaukee, remaining a short time in each of these localities. He then settled in Peoria County, in this State, and tried farming for a time, after which he went to Cincinnati, in 1839, and commenced the study of law. Being admitted to the bar in 1841, he practiced for a short time in that State, but in 1842 came to Illinois, and located at Carthage. There he remained until 1844, when he took up his residence in this city.

Before coming to Quincy however, his reputation as an able and profound lawyer had been established, and in 1851, he was elected to the bench of this circuit, In 1855 his great legal attainments received a more marked recognition, he being called to the Supreme Bench of the State. Previous to this he had also served one term in the Legislature, and in every position to which he was called by his friends and admirers, he was found not only equal to the emergency, but eminently the right man in the right place.

Retiring from the Supreme Bench, Judge Skinner became an active and influential leader in the Democratic party of Illinois, and although political honors were at all times within his grasp, he never advantaged himself of his opportunities in this respect. The past year, however, he was elected by the democracy of Adams County a delegate to the Convention to remodel the Constitution of Illinois, in which capacity he is now serving his constituents and the State in the most responsible position of that distinguished body, viz., as Chairman of the Judiciary Committee.

Quincy boasts no more distinguished or more valuable citizen than Judge Skinner. Full of public spirit and enterprise, he was among the earliest advocates of our railroad system, and having aided in the completion of the three roads that at present enter the city, he is now President of a fourth, the Quincy and Carthage Railroad, which by his energy and tact he has placed upon the road to speedy construction.

Generous, impulsive, and earnest, a zealous and untiring lawyer, a warm and devoted friend, and an uncomprising Democrat, such is Hon. O. C. Skinner.

AMOS GREEN, ESQ.,

OR "MEN OF MARK" IN QUINCY.

Few men have rendered more valuable service to Quincy than the subject of this sketch.

Amos Green was born in York Co., Pennsylvania, from whence he migrated to Quincy in 1836, being then not quite twenty-one years of age. Shortly after his arrival here he purchased a saw mill that stood on the site of the present C. B. & Q. R. R. freight depot. This enterprise not proving very successful or profitable, it was abandoned after one year's experience, and Mr. Green then followed the carpenter trade, at which he had served an apprenticeship. In 1845 he embarked in the lumber business, in which he was remarkably successful, building up an extensive trade, and acquiring large wealth. Mr. Green continued in this business here to within a few years, and is now senior partner of a firm operating in Chicago.

A man of marked sagacity and powerful mind, Mr. Green early took rank as an influential citizen, and has been identified with every public measure originated in Quincy. He served several years as a member of the City Council, and was one of the most efficient and valuable members of that body. His name has several times been mentioned in connection with other political positions, and although importuned to become a candidate, he has invariably declined. He was however the candidate for mayor on the Republican ticket in 1864, but the city being strongly democratic was defeated.

At all times an active and energetic citizen, Mr. Green has employed his wealth to improve and beautify the city in which he acquired it, and has erected some of the handsomest business structures in Quincy. In all respects he is one of its "men of mark."

CONCLUSION.

In concluding this review of the progress of Quincy from its first settlement, while apologising for our inability to make a more faithful and complete exhibit, we have no fears of a comparison with the history of any city of its age and size in the Union. If commercial power, prestige in manufactures, moral and social elevation, religious and educational advancement are the true indications of healthy and vigorous progress, then has Quincy reached an eminence among her metropolitan sisters that entitles her to bravely inscribe upon her escutcheon the name of "Model City," and claim it as her own. But the achievements of the future must dim even the brilliancy of her past record as a city. Great in everything worthy and noble, her thrifty inhabitants will continue their efforts to augment her power for good, and each succeeding year will find her steadily increasing in usefulness and wealth. The past should be an index of the future, and if in recording what has been accomplished by the genius and energy of her people in years gone by, those of to-day be nerved to consummate the work of giving Quincy a pre-eminent position among the commercial and manufacturing centers of the Union, then will we at least feel that this little volume was not published in vain.

WILLARD KEYES, Esq.,

OR, "MEN OF MARK" IN QUINCY.

The subject of this sketch has passed nearly half a century within the present limits of the city of Quincy, and in that period has watched her progress with a jealous eye.

Willard Keyes is a native of Vermont, where he was born in 1792. Leaving his native state in 1817, he proceeded to Prairie du Chien, where he remained one year and a half, being employed during that time in teaching the French settlers and half-breed Indians. Descending the river in the spring of 1820, after a voyage of two weeks Mr. Keyes landed at Clarksville, Mo. After a summer's experience with the fever and ague, he started on a tour of exploration with John Wood, whose acquaintance he formed about this time, going up the Illinois, and down the Mississippi river. Visiting St. Louis, he sold his raft and proceeded from there to Calhoun county in this state, and spent the winter teaching school. In the spring of 1824 he arrived in Quincy, and joined his friend, John Wood, who had previously settled here. Mr. Keyes at once erected a house, which was the second built upon the site of the present city of Quincy. From that time to the present day, he has manifested a deep interest in the prosperity of thecity, of which he helped lay the foundation. At present, advanced beyond the age alloted to man, he still views with pride the strides of our city in commerce, arts, and sciences. A pure christian and upright citizen, Willard Keyes is reverenced by the entire community as one of the "Fathers of Quincy," which he may be justly called.

INDEX.

face.................................... 3
Historical............................ 5
Manufacturing and Commercial
  Interests........................... 15

MANUFACTURES.

Flour 23
Tobacco............................... 29
Machine Shops..................... 33
Foundries............................ 35
Stoves................................. 36
Breweries............................ 41
Paper.................................. 42
Distilleries.......................... 54
Carriages............................ 55
Boiler and Sheet Iron Works 60
Gas..................................... 64
Wagons, Plows &c................ 71
Planing Mills...................... 72
Brick.................................. 73
Saddles and Harness............ 80
Ice..................................... 84
Agricultural Implements...... 95
Saw Mill............................ 112
Broom Factory................... 112
Printing............................. 115
Hair Work.......................... 115
Pork Packing...................... 118
Rectifiers........................... 121
Soda Factories.................... 121
Furniture........................... 124
Organs............................... 124
Fruit and Pickle Factory..... 127
Rope and Twine.................. 127
Book Binders..................... 129
Boots and Shoes.................. 129
Confectioners.................... 133
Marble Works.................... 133
Chairs............................... 137
Engraving.......................... 137
Match Factories................. 137
Tannery............................. 141
Hoop Skirt Manufacturers... 141
Horse Collars..................... 141
Blacksmiths....................... 145
Gunsmiths......................... 145
Coopers............................. 148

Baskets 148
Tin and Copper Workers..... 151
Soap, Candles &c................. 151
Merchant Tailoring............. 154
Photographers................... 154
Cigars................................ 157
Watchmakers and Jewelers.. 157
Bakers............................... 160
Baking Powder,................. 160
Bags.................................. 163
Miscellaneous Manufactures.. 163

MERCANTILE.

Dry Goods and Notions....... 167
Grocery Trade.................... 171
Hardware and Iron............. 174
Drugs................................ 175
Boots and Shoes................. 177
Books and Stationery.......... 179
Hats and Caps.................... 182
Millinery Goods................. 182
China, Glass, &c................. 184
Agricultural Implements,... 184
Clothing............................ 187
Carpets.............................. 187
Coal................................... 190
Coal Oil............................. 190
Fish Markets..................... 190
Flour and Feed.................. 193
Forwarding and Commission. 193
Furniture........................... 193
Grain................................. 195
Hides, Furs, Wool &c.......... 195
Leather.............................. 195
Liquors............................. 199
Musical Goods................... 199
Lumber, Shingles, Lath &c.. 202
Paints, Oils and Glass......... 202
Paper—Flat, Print &c......... 203
Salt................................... 203
Seeds................................. 203
Sewing Machines................ 203
Tinner's Stock................... 206
Tobacco Leaf..................... 206
Tobacco, Cigars &c.............. 206
Wall Paper and Shades....... 206
Miscellaneous.................... 209

THE ORPHANS.

St. Aloysius Society 46
Woodland Home 49
St. Mary's Hospital 77

The Rink 88
The Quincy Railroad Bridge 101
Hotels 213
Professional 215
The "Press." 219
Banking Institutions 225
Educational 230
Religious 236
Fire Department 243
Railroads 247
River Commerce 270
Horse Railway 256
Projected Railroads 270
Cemeteries 276
Executions 281
City Government 289
Conclusion 295

BIOGRAPHICAL SKETCHES.

Ex-Gov. John Wood 26
Hon. Thos. Jasper 31
Hon. Wm. A. Richardson 38
Hon. O. H. Browning 41
Hon. Maitland Boon 52
Hon. Jas. M. Pitman 57
J. K. VanDoorn, Esq. 62
H. V. Sullivan, Esq. 68
Gen. Jas. D. Morgan 74
Enoch Comstock, Esq. 81
Henry Root, Esq. 85
Chas. A. Savage, Esq. 92
Hon. C. A. Warren 97
Henry F. Joseph Ricker, Esq. 110
Hon. Alexander E. Wheat 113
C. M. Pomroy, Esq. 116
Geo. Adams, Esq. 119
Judge T. J. Mitchell 122
Wm. Steinwedell, Esq. 125
M. Jacobs, Esq. 128
Louis Buddee, Esq. 130
R. W. Gardner, Esq. 134
Capt. Michael Piggott 138

A. J. F. Provost, Esq. 142
F. H. Aldrich, Esq. 143
Col. M. M. Bane 146
N. D. Munson, Esq. 149
Wm. G. Ewing, Esq. 152
Col. J. B. Cahill 155
Col. C. H. Morton 158
Col. K. K. Jones 161
F. W. Meyer, Esq. 165
Robert Tillson, Esq. 169
Hon. Jackson Grimshaw 172
Aldo Sommer, Esq. 176
A. B. Kingsbury, Esq. 178
S. P. Bartlett, Esq. 180
Louis Miller, Esq. 183
Wm. B. Andrews, Esq. 185
Henry Allen, Esq. 188
Col. Joseph G. Rowland 191
Samuel E. Seger, Esq. 194
Gen. B. M. Prentiss 196
Newton Flagg, Esq. 200
Geo. W. Burns, Esq. 204
F. W. Jansen, Esq. 207
R. S. Benneson, Esq. 211
E. K. Stone, Esq. 214
W. H. Johnson, Esq. 217
Jas. Arthur, Esq. 223
Edward Wells, Esq. 228
Wm. Morris, Esq. 234
Chas. W. Keyes, Esq. 235
H. S. Osborn, Esq. 237
S. J. Lesem, Esq. 239
J. W. Brown, Esq. 241
Hon. B. F. Berrian 245
U. S. Penfield, Esq. 257
Wendelin Weber, Esq. 265
F. D. Schermerhorn, Esq. 268
J. D. Levy, Esq. 272
Capt. F. S. Lee 273
J. T. Bradford, Esq. 274
Henry Frank, Esq. 277
Austin Brooks, Esq. 279
N. Bushnell, Esq. 283
Hon. J. W. Singleton 285
E. H. Turner, Esq. 288
Hon. Thomas Redmond 292
Hon. O. C. Skinner 294
Amos Green, Esq. 296
Willard Keyes, Esq. 299

www.ingramcontent.com/pod-product-compliance
Lightning Source LLC
Chambersburg PA
CBHW030817230426
43667CB00008B/1265